A TASTE OF
Jackson Hole II

...all new recipes from old favorite restaurants,
plus 20 new restaurants

by

Christine Goodman

Christine Goodman
P.O. Box 3308
Jackson, Wyoming 83001

Additional copies may be obtained by contacting Christine Goodman. For your convenience, order forms are included in the back of this book.

Cover and Illustrations by
Chuck Johnston

ISBN: 0-9633566-1-5

Printed by
Myers-Frank, Printers
Shelley, Idaho

For Erin

Thank you for being such a wonderful daughter!

I have so many people to thank for making this book possible. First, of course, I want to gratefully acknowledge and thank all the chefs and restaurant owners who so graciously took time from their very demanding and busy schedules to share some of their recipes with us. Without their recipes, there wouldn't be a book!

And a very big thank you to so many others. Thank you from the bottom of my heart to Mike Palazzolo and the Chandless Computer Group, to Thana Saycocie and Main Event Computers, and to David Swift and Colleen Thompson for being so supportive and helpful to me during my many computer crises! And thank you, Cathie Burkland, for believing in me.

Thank you very much to my good friend, Wendy Sexton, for proofreading all the recipes and for putting together the Index! And thank you to my brother, Chuck, and sister-in-law, Deborah for being so loving, supportive and helpful.

A special thank you to Pete and Jacque Cook at The Wine Loft for making this second printing of *Taste of Jackson Hole II* possible, with the wonderful contribution of wine pairings for so many of the recipes.

I want to especially thank my father, Chuck Johnston, for once again creating the wonderful drawings which make this book special.

With love and gratitude,

Christine

PARTICIPATING RESTAURANTS

Alpenhof Bistro
The Alpenhof Lodge
Teton Village
307/733-3242

Amangani Grill
Amangani
East Gros Ventre Butte
307/734-7333

Anthony's Italian Restaurant
Jackson
307/733-3717

Atrium
Snow King Resort
Jackson
307/733-5200

Beantown Cafe
Jackson
307/734-4457

Betty Rock Cafe
Jackson
307/733-0747

Blue Lion Restaurant
Jackson
307/733-3912

Cadillac Grille
Jackson
307/733-3279

Calico Italian Restaurant & Bar
Teton Village Road
307/733-2460

The Downtowner
Jackson
307/733-2877

The Granary
Spring Creek Ranch
East Gros Ventre Butte
307/733-8833

Grateful Bread
Jackson
307/734-1253

Jenny Lake Lodge Dining Room
Grand Teton National Park
307/543-2811

Koshu Wine Bar
Jackson
307/733-5283

Lame Duck Chinese Restaurant
Jackson
307/733-4311

Mangy Moose Restaurant & Saloon
Teton Village
307/733-4913

Merry Piglets Mexican Grill
Jackson
307/733-2966

Million Dollar Cowboy Steakhouse
Jackson
307/733-4790

Mural Dining Room
Jackson Lake Lodge
Grand Teton National Park
307/543-2811

Nani's Genuine Pasta House
Jackson
307/733-3888

Off Broadway Grill
Jackson
307/733-9777

Old Yellowstone Garage
Jackson
307/734-6161

The Peaks Restaurant
Signal Mountain Lodge
Grand Teton National Park
307/543-2831

The Range
Jackson
307/733-5481

Rising Sage Cafe
National Museum of Wildlife Art
Jackson
307/733-8649

Snake River Brewery
Jackson
307/739-2337

Snake River Grill
Jackson
307/733-0557

Stagecoach Grill
Wilson
307/733-6610

Stiegler's Austrian Restaurant & Bar
Teton Village Road
307/733-1071

Strutting Grouse Restaurant
Jackson Hole Golf & Tennis
307/733-7788

Terroir Restaurant
Jackson
307/739-2500

Teton Pines Restaurant
Teton Pines Resort & Country Club
Teton Village Road
307/733-1005

• •

Huckleberry Mountain
Jackson   307/739-9313
Toll Free   800/272-2999
www.huckleberrymtn.com

Jackson Hole Buffalo Meat Company
Jackson   307/733-8343
Toll Free   800/543-6328
www.jhbuffalomeat.com

Spice Merchant
Oriental Cooking Secrets
Jackson   307/733-7811
Toll Free   800/551-5999
www.orientalcookingsecrets.com

TABLE OF CONTENTS

PART I

Full Menu / Featured Restaurants

PART II

Selected Recipes Restaurants

PART III

Great Cooks I Know....
And a Few Recipes of My Own!

RECIPES BY MENU CATEGORY

APPETIZERS

SOUPS

SALADS

ENTREES

SIDES

BREADS / BAKED GOODS

DESSERTS

PART I

Full Menu / Featured Restaurants

chas

Located high above the town of Jackson, perched on the crest of East Gros Ventre Butte, Amangani enjoys magnificent views of the Snake River Range and the Grand Teton Mountains to the north. Its name born out of Sanskrit and the Native American language of the Shoshone, Amangani means "peaceful home" (Aman is "peaceful" in Sanskrit; gani means "home" in Shoshone).

Amangani is a magnificent resort hotel, as beautiful and unique as its name. With an exterior of Oklahoma sandstone, its interior is rich and warm with clear-heart redwood and sandstone, furnishings of rattan, woven cowhide and terrazzo, art and antiques reflective of the West.

Amangani's Grill is exquisite and cozy with its wood-burning fireplace and use of rare woods....and of course, a spectacular view. Before dinner, guests can enjoy refreshments in their stunning Lounge with its two-story window wall, or on the terrace; either affording an incredible setting for sunset watchers!

Chef Thomas Stevens has the pleasure of making sure guests of the Grill enjoy their dining experience as much as they enjoy their beautiful surroundings. With his great creativity and talent, Chef Thomas develops dishes which are unique and absolutely delicious!

MENU FOR FOUR

Miso Broth
with Shitake Lemongrass Dumpling

recommended wine - dry fume blanc with a pineapple-citrus body
Grgich Hills Fume Blanc

Fire Roasted Prawns
with Tropical BBQ Sauce
and Grilled Pineapple Salsa

recommended wine - dry gerwurztraminer with honey and vanilla
Trimbach Gerwurztraminer

Nectarine-Blueberry Deep Dish Cobbler
Honey-Lavender Ice Cream
with Lavender Meringues

recommended wine - sweet, nutty dessert wine with big flavor
San Felice Vin Santo - Italia

Chef Thomas Stevens
Pastry Chef Toby Bauer

Wine pairings by The Wine Loft

MISO BROTH with
SHITAKE LEMONGRASS DUMPLING

Serves 4

This soup should be made one day ahead, so the flavors can develop fully.

In soup pot, heat...	2	tablespoons	*sesame oil*
	2	tablespoons	*canola oil*
Add...	1/4	cup	*fresh ginger,* peeled, chopped
(mire poix)	1	small	*red onion,* chopped
	1	whole	*lemongrass bulb,* peeled, chopped
	2	tablespoons	*garlic,* chopped
	4	tablespoons	*cilantro,* chopped
Sweat (cook) until onions are translucent. Add...	1/2	cup	*shoyu*
	1/4	cup	*mirin vinegar*
	2	teaspoons	*Szechwan peppercorns*
	1	teaspoon	*coriander seeds*
Reduce by half.			

Fold in...	4	cups	*red miso paste**

Fully incorporate with the
mire poix, stirring constantly,
about 2 minutes.

Be careful not to burn the paste. Add **one gallon cold water** and bring to a slight simmer. Remove from heat. Strain and cool. Refrigerate until use. To serve, place Shitake Lemongrass Dumplings in broth and reheat to a slight simmer. DO NOT boil the soup.

*Available in gourmand section of grocers. See Spice Merchant, Participating Restaurants index.

Shitake Lemongrass Dumplings

For this recipe, you will need...	4	pieces	*wonton skins*
In sauté pan, heat...	1/2	teaspoon	*sesame oil*
	1/2	teaspoon	*red chile oil*

| Add and caramelize... | 1 | cup | *shitake mushrooms* |
| | | | stems removed, julienned |

Add...	3	tablespoons	*green onions,*
			white part only, finely sliced
	1	teaspoon	*garlic,* minced
	¹/₂	teaspoon	*fresh ginger,* minced
	1	tablespoon	*lemongrass,* minced
	1	tablespoon	*red pepper,*
			finely diced
Sauté briefly. Deglaze with...	2	tablespoons	*sake*

Cool mixture. Brush a *wonton skin* with egg wash and place one tablespoon of mixture into it. Fold corners in and press edges to seal. Repeat for three more dumplings. Refrigerate dumplings until ready to reheat miso broth. Place dumplings gently into both and bring to a slight simmer. Serve.

FIRE ROASTED PRAWNS
with TROPICAL BBQ SAUCE
and GRILLED PINEAPPLE SALSA
Serves 4

Great for entertaining! By making the BBQ sauce and Pineapple Salsa early in the day, pulling it all together at dinner time will be a snap.

For this recipe, you will need...	12	U-10	*pacific prawns*
			(jumbo shrimp are fine)
	12		*bamboo skewers*
	1	tablespoon	*red chile oil*

Peel prawns, keeping tail end on; devein. Hold the tail straight and slide a bamboo skewer through the prawn. [This will keep the prawn straight after grilling.] Brush prawns with chile oil and season with salt and pepper. Set aside.

In sauté pan, over medium flame, heat...	1	teaspoon	*sesame oil*
Add and sauté for 30 seconds...	1	tablespoon	*fresh ginger,* crushed
	1	teaspoon	*garlic,* minced
Add and reduce...	1	tablespoon	*rice vinegar*

Add...	$1/2$	cup	*orange juice,* fresh squeezed
	$1/2$	cup	*pineapple juice*
	2	tablespoons	*lime juice,* fresh squeezed
	3	tablespoons	*hoisin sauce*
	1	tablespoon	*sweet chile sauce*
	1	tablespoon	*clover honey*
	1	tablespoon	*sesame seeds,* toasted
	1	teaspoon	*soy sauce*
			coarse sea salt, to taste
			black pepper, finely ground, to taste

Simmer for 5 minutes and strain.

Place skewered prawns on hot grill for 2 minutes per side. Immediately after removing prawns from grill, brush with Tropical BBQ Sauce on both sides. The sauce should slightly caramelize. To serve, top prawns with Grilled Pineapple Salsa, drizzle the plate with a little of the BBQ sauce and garnish with a sprig of *cilantro*. Chef Stevens suggests sticky rice as a nice simple side dish.

Grilled Pineapple Salsa

For this recipe, you will need...	1	whole	*Maui pineapple,* peeled

Slice peeled pineapple vertically into $5^{1}/_{4}$" strips, remove core off the edge. Place strips on hot grill and sear, about one minute per side. Remove from grill and dice into $^{1}/_{4}$" x $^{1}/_{4}$" cubes.

Toss pineapple cubes with...	2	tablespoons	*apple cider*
	1	tablespoon	*green peppercorns,* minced

3	tablespoons	*red pearl onions,* thinly sliced
3	tablespoons	*red pepper,* finely diced

NECTARINE-BLUEBERRY DEEP DISH COBBLER with HONEY-LAVENDER ICE CREAM and LAVENDER MERINGUES

Amangani Grill makes all their own ice cream. They have a lot of fun creating some very unique flavors. One of them, a Peach-Sage ice cream, uses the fresh wild sage that grows all around Jackson. Chefs Tom and Toby encourage you to use the base recipe for making your own ice cream....just leave out the lavendar and substitute whatever flavors, berries or fruit you wish. Enjoy!

For the pie, in bowl combine...

6	medium	*nectarines,* pitted, sliced
1/2	pint	*blueberries,* rinsed
3/4	cup	*sugar*
3	tablespoons	*cornstarch*
3	tablespoons	*fresh lemon juice*

Stir well; place in 8" x 8" baking dish.

Bake in **preheated** 350° oven for 35 minutes until a thick blue syrup has formed and the nectarines are cooked through. Allow to cool. Scoop pie mixture into 4 individual pie dishes or ramekins, or in one 6" casserole dish, filling only to three quarters full. Refrigerate for up to three days until needed.

To assemble: warm pies in oven or microwave. Place one scoop Honey-Lavender Ice Cream on top of pie mixture. Top with Lavender Meringue.

Honey-Lavender Ice Cream

In small saucepan, combine...

1	quart	*half and half*
1 1/2	teaspoons	*dried lavender buds*
	OR	

	1 tablespoon	*fresh lavender buds*

Place over medium-low heat and begin warming.

In mixing bowl large enough to act as double boiler on saucepan, combine...	10	*egg yolks* (reserve whites for meringues)
	1 ¹/₂ cups	*honey*

Place bowl over warming half and half.

Slowly warm until eggs reach 110°. Pour half and half mixture over eggs and honey, whisking slowly. When combined, allow to steep for 10 minutes; strain through fine sieve and allow to cool either in ice bath or in refrigerator overnight or until cold. Churn in ice cream maker using their instructions. Freeze.

Lavender Meringues

In mixing bowl, combine...	10	*egg whites*
	³/₄ cup	*sugar*
Whip until quadrupled in volume, is shiny and ribbon like. Whip in...	1 tablespoon	*fresh lavender buds* chopped
	OR	
	1 ¹/₂ teaspoons	*dried lavender buds* crushed

Pipe meringue onto parchment-lined baking sheet in whatever size pies or pie you are making. Bake in **preheated** 225° oven for 3 hours. Pull from oven and allow to crisp at room temperature for 30 minutes. Use immediately or place in airtight container until needed.

chas

Anthony's Italian Restaurant was opened, at its present location, in February 1977. In September of 1980, Anthony Wall, chef/manager since 1977, assumed ownership of the business. In 1983, Anthony's expanded, taking over the adjacent storefront and adding a full bar and waiting room. Mr. Wall, who is also an antiques dealer, has decorated the bar with antique beer and liquor advertisements, as well as art and memorabilia acquired from various trips to Italy.

Managers Pete Wiswell and Stan Wood and their experienced staff, most of whom have worked there for at least 10 years, emphasize consistency and a fun, informal atmosphere which could only be called "Italian style."

All of Anthony's dinners include freshly baked garlic bread, minestrone soup or seafood chowder, salad, entree and dessert, complemented by a wine list which includes an extensive selection of Italian wines. Of course, espresso and cappuccino are available after dinner.

MENU FOR SIX

Fried Eggplant
with Marinara Sauce

recommended wine ~ very light, crisp, smooth pinot gris
Campanile Pinot Grigio

Minestrone

Anthony's House Salad
with Italian Dressing

Garlic Bread

Linguine con Vongole/Calamari

recommended wine ~ light bodied Tuscan red with berry flavor
Canaleto Montepulciano

Chef Anthony Wall

Wine pairings by The Wine Loft

FRIED EGGPLANT with MARINARA SAUCE   Serves 6

| For this recipe, you will need... | 1 | large | *eggplant* |
| | | | (or 2 small) |

Peel, then cut eggplants into $1/4$" to $3/8$" thick slices. Place slices in deep pan completely covered with cold water to which a small handful of salt has been added. Store in refrigerator.

In shallow pan, mix together...	$1/2$	cup	*flour*
	$1/2$	cup	*bread crumbs*
	$1/2$	cup	*parmesan cheese,*
			finely grated
	1	teaspoon	*salt*
	1	teaspoon	*pepper*
	1	pinch	*leaf oregano*
	1	pinch	*basil*
	1	pinch	*garlic powder*

| To complete recipe, you will need... | 2 | whole | *eggs,* beaten |
| | | | *vegetable oil* |

Remove eggplant from the refrigerator, drain off the water and pat dry. Dip each slice completely in *beaten eggs*, then press into bread crumb mixture. Coat both sides well. Fry in a deep fryer or in a half inch of *vegetable oil*, turning at least once, until golden brown. Serve with Marinara Sauce.

Marinara Sauce

In large saucepan, combine...	$1/4$	cup	*extra virgin olive oil*
			heated
Add...	6	cloves	*garlic,* minced
	1	large	*yellow onion,* finely
			diced

Sauté until onions are translucent.

Add to mixture...	1	large	*green pepper,* finely diced
	1	large	*red pepper,* finely diced
Sauté for 3-4 minutes, stirring constantly to prevent garlic from burning.			

Add and simmer for 3-4 minutes...	$^1/_2$	cup	*dry red wine*

Add and simmer over low heat for 45 to 60 minutes...	32	ounces	*canned tomatoes,* (crushed)
	3	whole	*bay leaves*
	1	teaspoon	*dried oregano*
	1	teaspoon	*dried basil*
	1	teaspoon	*salt*
	1	teaspoon	*black pepper*

If the tomato product used was extremely thick, you may want to add a little water to thin the sauce to the correct consistency. This recipe makes a little over one quart.

MINESTRONE

Serves 6

In small stock pot, combine...	$^1/_2$	cup	*extra virgin olive oil*
	4	large	*garlic cloves,* minced
	1	large	*carrot,* diced
	1	large	*celery stalk,* diced
	1	medium	*red pepper,* diced
	1	medium	*yellow onion,* diced
	$^1/_2$	small head	*green cabbage,* sliced
	1	large	*potato,* diced
	3	medium	*fresh tomatoes,* diced (with the juice)
Cook until onions are translucent.			

Add to mixture and cook for
another 2-3 minutes...

1	large pinch	*dried basil*
1	large pinch	*dried oregano*
1	teaspoon	*salt*
1	teaspoon	*black pepper*
1/2	cup	*lentils* (soaked over-night in water)

Add and bring to a boil...   2   quarts   *vegetable stock**

Remove soup from heat.   Check seasoning.

Serve with freshly grated...   *parmesan or romano cheese*

Homemade is best, or use good quality canned (with no MSG).

ANTHONY'S HOUSE SALAD
with ITALIAN DRESSING

Serves 6

Break off leaves and tear by hand,
wash and drain...

1	head	*romaine*
1	head	*red leaf lettuce* (or baby spring greens)

Shred and mix with lettuce in
large wooden bowl...

2	large	*carrots*
1/2	small	*red cabbage*

Garnish with tomato wedges and croutons. Dress with Anthony's Italian Dressing.

Anthony's Italian Dressing

Whisk together until well blended...	1 1/8	cup	*extra virgin olive oil*
	1/2	cup	*white balsamic vinegar**
	1	tablespoon	*dijon mustard*
	4	large	*garlic cloves,* minced
	1	teaspoon	*cracked black pepper*
	1	pinch	*salt*
Fold in...	1/4	pound	*blue cheese,* finely crumbled

*You can substitute apple cider vinegar.

LINGUINE con VONGOLE/CALAMARI
Serves 6

For this recipe, you will need...	6-8	cups	*linguine,* cooked al dente
In large sauté pan or iron skillet, heat...	4	tablespoons	*butter*
	4	tablespoons	*olive oil*
Add... Sauté and stir constantly until lightly browned (don't let it burn!).	6	large	*garlic cloves,* minced
Slice diagonally into 1" slices and add to skillet...	1	cup	*green onions*
Saute until soft (about 2 minutes). Deglaze with...	1/4	cup	*dry white wine*

| Add... | 1/2 | pound | *calamari,* sliced (rings and tentacles) |
| | 1/2 | pound | *clams,* chopped |

Sauté for 3-4 minutes.
Add additional...

| | 1/2 | cup | *dry white wine* |

Simmer until wine reduces.

Add...	1	cup	*heavy cream*
	4	ounces	*parmesan cheese,* finely grated
			cracked black pepper and salt to taste

Stir well and cook for
1-2 minutes more.

Serve over al dente linguine with Garlic Bread.

Garlic Bread

| For this recipe you will need... | 1 | loaf | *crusty french bread,* split lengthwise |

In small saucepan, melt...	1/2	cup	*butter*
	1/2	cup	*olive oil*
Add...	2	tablespoons	*roasted garlic,* chopped
		pinch	*salt*

Brush open faces of french bread with garlic butter. Broil just long enough to lightly brown.

[To roast garlic, place garlic cloves, glazed with small amount of olive oil, on baking sheet. Bake in **preheated** 350° oven for 15 minutes, until slightly golden.]

chas

SNOW KING RESORT

The Atrium Restaurant and Rafferty's are part of the Snow King Resort, a 204 room, full-service hotel, set at the base of Snow King Mountain. Rafferty's specializes in its extraordinary Sunday champagne brunch. In addition to serving lunch and dinner, another specialty of the Atrium is its elaborate breakfast buffet served daily in the open, plant-filled mezzanine of Snow King Resort.

The Snow King Resort, with its new activity center, is a hub for local events and actvities, as well as an ideal environment for groups of any size to convene for conferences and symposiums. The activity center fulfills a multitude of uses. It is not only an ice rink, but it is also an exhibit hall, a sports arena and a concert hall. Any time of the year, there is always something happening at SKR, to the delight of local and visitors alike!

BRUNCH FOR SIX

Oysters Rockefeller

recommended wine ~ sparkling wine with light spice and vanilla
Moet Chandon 'White Star'

Fruit Salad with Grand Marnier

Spring Mix with Fresh Raspberries and Balsamic Vinaigrette

Sole Florentine with Mornay Sauce

recommended wine ~ white burgandy with hint of dryness, vanilla and plum
Louis Jadot Pouilly Fuisse

Roasted Beef Tenderloin with Bourbon Shitake Mushrooms

recommended wine ~ big, deep, fruitful cabernet
Jordan Cabernet Sauvignon

Russian Cream with Boysenberries

Huckleberry Cobbler

Chef Tim Cotten

Wine pairings by The Wine Loft

OYSTERS ROCKEFELLER

Serves 4

For this recipe, you will need...	18-24		*Blue Point Oysters*
In saucepan, over medium heat, add...	2	tablespoons	*butter*
	$1/_4$	cup	*bacon,* chopped
	$1/_4$	cup	*shallots,* minced
	1	teaspoon	*garlic,* minced
Cook until shallots are translucent.			

Add...	$1/_4$	cup	*pernod*
	3	cups	*fresh spinach,* stems removed, chopped
Cook until spinach is wilted. Add and mix well...	$1/_4$	cup	*heavy cream*
			salt and pepper to taste
Remove from heat; let cool.			

To complete recipe, you will need...		*rock salt*
		lemon wedges

Remove from heat and cool. Put spoonful of mixture over oysters to cover. Cover baking sheet with a layer of rock salt. Arrange oysters on rock salt. Bake in **preheated** 450° oven for 8-10 minutes. Remove from oven and put a tablespoon of Hollandaise atop each oyster. Put back in oven for one minute, until glazed. Serve on rock salt with lemon wedges.

Hollandaise

In top of double boiler, combine...	6	large	*egg yolks*
	1	tablespoon	*fresh lemon juice*
	1	tablespoon	*dry white wine*
	$1/_2$	teaspoon	*tabasco sauce*
	1	pinch	*white pepper*
Cook and stir over simmering water until thickened slightly.			

While whisking constantly,
  slowly add...   1¹/₂   **cups**   *clarified butter,*
                                                          melted

Stir to desired consistency. Remove from heat.

FRUIT SALAD with GRAND MARNIER   Serves 6

In large bowl, combine...   ¹/₂   **cup**   *fresh pineapple,*
                                                         cubed
                                  ¹/₂   **cup**   *honeydew melon,*
                                                         cubed
                                  ¹/₂   **cup**   *cantaloupe,* cubed
                                  ¹/₂   **cup**   *strawberries,*
                                                         quartered
                                  ¹/₂   **cup**   *kiwi,* diced

In separate bowl, whisk together... 1   **cup**   *fresh orange juice*
                                  ¹/₄   **cup**   *Grand Marnier*
                                  ¹/₄   **cup**   *powdered sugar*

Toss mixture with fruit. Cover and refrigerate to macerate for 2 hours.

SPRING MIX with FRESH RASPBERRIES
and BALSAMIC VINAIGRETTE

Serves 6

In salad bowl, toss together...	1/2	pound	*spring greens*
	1	cup	*fresh raspberries*
	1/2	cup	*red onion,* julienned
	1/2	cup	*black olives,* sliced
	1	cup	*shitake mushrooms,* sliced

Just before serving, drizzle with Balsamic Vinaigrette and toss well.

Balsamic Vinaigrette

Whisk together...	1/2	cup	*balsamic vinegar*
	1	cup	*pureed raspberries*
	2	tablespoons	*honey*
	1	tablespoon	*roasted garlic,* minced
	1	tablespoon	*shallots,* minced
	1	tablespoon	*fresh basil,* finely chopped
	1	teaspoon	*black pepper*
Whisk in...	1	cup	*extra virgin olive oil*

SOLE FLORENTINE with MORNAY SAUCE   Serves 6

For this recipe, you will need...	2	pounds	*sole filets,* rolled
In saucepan, over medium heat, add...	2	tablespoons	*butter*
	1	cup	*mushrooms,* sliced
	1	tablespoon	*shallots,* minced
	1	teaspoon	*garlic,* minced
Cook until mushrooms are tender.			

Add...	3	cups	*fresh spinach*
Stir and cook until spinach is cooked, about 1 minute.			

Spread spinach mixture in buttered baking dish to cover bottom. Arrange rolled up *sole filets* on top of spinach. Drizzle a little *melted butter* over the top and sprinkle with *salt and pepper to taste.* Bake in **preheated** 350° oven until sole is cooked through, about 20-25 minutes. To serve spoon Mornay Sauce over top of each filet of sole.

Mornay Sauce

In heavy saucepan, combine...	1/2	cup	*cream sherry*
	2	tablespoons	*onion,* finely minced
	4	small	*bay leaves*
Simmer for 10 minutes. Remove bay leaf.			

Add and bring to a boil...	2	cups	*heavy cream*
	1	pinch	*nutmeg*
			salt and pepper to taste
Lower heat and whisk in...	1/2	cup	*parmesan cheese*
	1/2	cup	*jack cheese,* shredded

Simmer over lowest heat until thickened to desired consistency.

ROASTED BEEF TENDERLOIN
with BOURBON SHITAKE MUSHROOMS   Serves 6

For this recipe, you will need...	1	2¹/₂ pound	*beef tenderloin* center cut
	1	tablespoon	*garlic,* minced
	2	tablespoons	*fresh thyme,* leaves only, chopped

Trim tenderloin of any fat and remove silverskin. Rub meat all over with garlic and coat with thyme. In hot skillet with oil, sear *tenderloin* on all sides. Remove from pan and place in a **preheated** 350° oven to roast for about 25-30 minutes, or until done (internal temperature of 115°-120° for rare or medium rare), while preparing sauce.

Remove from oven. Let rest for minutes before slicing. Serve with Bourbon Shitake Mushrooms.

Bourbon Shitake Mushrooms

In skillet, over medium heat, add...	2	tablespoons	*butter*
	2	medium	*red onions,* julienned
	1	tablespoon	*roasted garlic,* minced
	1	tablespoon	*fresh thyme,* chopped
Sauté about 2-3 minutes. Onions should still be firm.			

Add...	1	pound	*shitake mushrooms,* sliced
	¹/₄	cup	*sour mash whiskey*
	1	teaspoon	*salt and black pepper to taste*
Sauté until mushrooms are tender. Do not overcook.			

RUSSIAN CREAM with BOYSENBERRIES   Serves 6

In small bowl, combine...	$^1/_2$	cup	*cold water*
	4	teaspoons	*powdered gelatin*
Set aside.			

In stainless steel bowl, combine...	2	cups	*sour cream*
	1	cup	*heavy cream*
	$^2/_3$	cup	*sugar*
	2	tablespoons	*fresh lemon juice*
	$^1/_2$	teaspoon	*vanilla*
Place bowl over boiling water.			
Stir until cream is warm. Add...			*gelatin mixture*

Cook, stirring constantly until gelatin dissolves. Pour into serving bowl. Chill for 4 hours.

In bowl, toss together...	2	cups	*boysenberries*
	$^1/_2$	cup	*sugar*

Serve Russian Cream topped with boysenberries. Garnish with whipped cream.

HUCKLEBERRY COBBLER   Serves 6-8

Delicious by itself, it is even better served with real vanilla ice cream!

In saucepan, combine...	4	cups	*huckleberries**
	2	cups	*sugar*
	1	cup	*cranberry juice*
	2	tablespoons	*fresh lemon juice*
Bring to a boil, stirring occasionally.			

In small bowl, combine...	$^1/_4$	cup	*water*
	$^1/_4$	cup	*cornstarch*

While stirring, slowly add cornstarch mixture to berries. Cook over low heat until thick, about 10 minutes. Pour into a 8" x 8" baking dish and cover with Streusel Topping. Bake in **preheated** 350° oven for one hour or until golden brown. Serve warm with vanilla ice cream.

Available at Huckleberry Mountain (see Participating Restaurants Index, page v).

Streusel Topping

In mixing bowl, combine...

2	cups	*flour*
1	cup	*brown sugar*
1	teaspoon	*cinnamon*
$1/2$	pound	*butter,* softened

Mix until well blended. There will be lumps.

In the mid-seventies a charming old home was converted into the Blue Lion Restaurant. Ned Brown became the proud owner of the Blue Lion in 1978 after spending a summer in Jackson Hole enjoying his love of outdoor sports. Ned had traveled to numerous Rocky Mountain resorts looking for the perfect area to pursue his dream of owning his own restaurant.

Florice Brown, Ned's mother, played an influential part in developing the Blue Lion's French cuisine. Some of her recipes have been used consistently over the past 22 years, including the fudge sauce which adorns one of the locals' favorite desserts — Mud Pie!

Ned and his wife, Sheri, along with their chef, Tim Labassi, have incorporated the French cuisine into a more Continental style menu, stressing the importance of using only the freshest ingredients available. The Blue Lion even has its own herb garden on the premises. Fresh fish is flown in daily, and free range veal is featured on the menu. Lighter, full-flavored sauces and salsas accompany most entrees, which include elk, lamb, charbroiled steaks, poultry, seafood, and vegetarian dishes. Home baked breads and desserts are prepared daily. Creative cuisine at its finest!

With a tree shaded patio for summer dining, and an upstairs dining room for private parties and large groups, the Blue Lion is truly a locals' favorite.

FEATURED RECIPES

Spinach and Smoked Chicken Salad

recommended wine ⁓ very dry, oaky, buttery chardonnay
Chateau Souverain Chardonnay

Southwestern Duck Cakes

recommended wine ⁓ very light, fruit-forward pinot noir
Duck Pond Pinot Noir

Tournedos au Bleu

recommended wine ⁓ dry, rich, full-bodied cabernet sauvignon
Groth Cabernet Sauvignon

Thai Shrimp Linguine

recommended wine ⁓ pinot grigio with light vanilla and hint of spice
King Estate Pinot Gris

Braised Halibut Mediterranean

recommended wine ⁓ big, berry-flavored merlot
Clos Du Val Merlot

Chef Tim Libassi

Wine pairings by The Wine Loft

SPINACH and SMOKED CHICKEN SALAD   Serves 4-5

Grilled chicken, smoked duck, or marinated grilled beef steaks can be substituted in this salad.

For this recipe, you will need...	1	pound	*smoked chicken breast,* skin removed and sliced
	1	large	*red pepper,* julienned
	1	cup	*mushrooms,* sliced
	1/2	cup	*red onion,* thinly sliced
	1 1/2	cups	*mandarin oranges,* drained
	1	cup	*croutons* (optional)

| Rinse, drain well and tear into pieces... | 1 | pound | *fresh spinach* |

Portion out spinach on serving plates, arrange vegetables and smoked chicken over spinach. Drizzle with Sesame Vinaigrette and garnish with croutons if desired.

Sesame Vinaigrette

In mixing bowl, whisk together until smooth...	1 1/4	cups	*rice vinegar*
	1/3	cup	*soy sauce*
	3	tablespoons	*brown sugar*
	1/4	cup	*lemon juice*
	3	tablespoons	*garlic,* minced

| While whisking, slowly add... | 1 | cup | *sesame oil* |
| | 1 1/4 | cups | *vegetable oil* |

| Add... | 1/4 | cup | *scallions or chives,* chopped |
| | 1/3 | cup | *sesame seeds,* toasted *salt and pepper to taste* |

Whisk again before serving if vinaigrette has separated.

SOUTHWESTERN DUCK CAKES

Serves 6-8

This recipe is great for enertaining as most of the preparation can be done ahead of time, even the day before! This recipe is also delicious made with chicken or pheasant.

In a large mixing bowl, combine...

1	pound	*ground duck*
1/3	whole	*red pepper,* minced
1/3	whole	*red onion,* minced
1	whole	*jalapeno,* minced (seeds removed)
3	tablespoons	*cilantro,* chopped
1	tablespoon	*garlic,* minced
1	tablespoon	*chives,* chopped
1/2	tablespoon	*cumin*
1/2	tablespoon	*coriander*
1/2	tablespoon	*chili powder*
2	tablespoons	*mayonnaise*
2/3	cup	*bread crumbs* *salt and pepper to taste*

After thoroughly blending above ingredients, add...

2		*egg whites,* whipped until stiff

Form mixture into cakes (can be made ahead to this point). Roll cakes in bread crumbs, sauté in medium hot skillet until golden. Bake in **preheated** 350° oven for 8 to 10 minutes to finish. Serve with Chipotle Mayonnaise.

Chipotle Mayonnaise

In food processor or blender, blend until smooth...

3	whole	*eggs*
1 1/2	tablespoons	*garlic,* crushed (2 large cloves)
3-5		*chipotle pepper,* seeded, stems removed
1	tablespoon	*lemon juice*

With machine running, slowly			
add...	1¹/₂	cups	*olive oil*
Followed by...	¹/₄	bunch	*cilantro*
			salt to taste

TOURNEDOS au BLEU

Serves 4

For this recipe, you will need...	2	tablespoons	*olive oil*
	4	6-8 ounces	*beef tenderloin filets*

In medium hot skillet, brown on both sides. Remove to **preheated** 400° oven to roast to desired doneness. Filets can also be grilled!

In same pan, add...	1	tablespoon	*olive oil*
	3	tablespoons	*shallots,* minced
	6-8		*artichoke hearts,* quartered

Sauté until shallots are translucent.

Add...	1	cup	*brandy*
Flame, let alcohol burn off.			
Add...	1¹/₄	cups	*veal stock**
Reduce by three quarters			

Add...	1	cup	*heavy cream*
	1	teaspoon	*dijon mustard*
Reduce to sauce consistency.			

Stir in to melt...	2	ounces	*Danish bleu cheese*
Add and heat through...	4-6	ounces	*snow crabmeat,* drained
			salt and pepper to taste

Serve immediately, draping tournedos with sauce. Note that this sauce can be made ahead, adding a little cream and stock when reheating.

For richness of the sauce, the quality of the stock is important. Canned stock can be substituted, but it won't be the same. Homemade chicken stock would be a preferable substitute. Veal stock can be made the same as beef stock, simply substitute veal bones; see index for recipe.

THAI SHRIMP LINGUINI

Any vegetables can be substituted in this dish; and the amount of sauce and cilantro can be varied to your own taste. Spiciness of the dish can be controlled by the amount of sauce and ginger used.

For this recipe you will need...	4-6	cups	*linguine,* cooked al dente
In skillet, over medium high heat, add...	2	tablespoons	*olive oil*
Heat and add...	1¼	pounds	*shrimp,* peeled and deveined
	3	tablespoons	*garlic,* chopped
	2	tablespoons	*fresh ginger,* chopped
	1½	whole	*red peppers,* seeded, julienned
	12		*artichoke hearts,* quartered
Sauté until shrimp are turning white, but are still translucent in seam along back.			
Add...	1	small bunch	*green onions,* chopped
	⅓	cup	*fresh cilantro,* chopped
	1	cup	*Thai Sauce*

Toss together and serve.

Thai Sauce

In food processor or blender, combine...	1/2	4 oz. can	*Panang red curry paste*
	3	tablespoons	*rice vinegar*
	6	tablespoons	*fresh lime juice* (about 4 limes)
	1/2	cup	*soy sauce*
Blend well.			

With machine running, add...	1/2	cup	*sesame oil*

BRAISED HALIBUT MEDITERRANEAN   Serves 4

In small bowl, mix together...	1	cup	*sundried tomatoes* (in oil) drained
(vegetable mixture)	1	cup	*artichoke hearts,* chopped
	1/2	cup	*kalamata olives,* cut into quarters
	1/2	cup	*green olives,* cut into quarters
	2	tablespoons	*capers*
	1/4	cup	*balsamic vinegar*
Set aside.			

Dredge in flour...	4	6-8 ounces	*halibut filets*
In large sauté pan, heat...	2	tablespoons	*olive oil*
Sear halibut on one side; remove to roasting pan, seared side up.			

In same saute pan, add			
and cook one minute...	1	**tablespoon**	*garlic,* minced
	1	**tablespoon**	*shallots,* minced
Add...			*vegetable mixture*
	1	**cup**	*dry white wine*
	¹/₂	**cup**	*vegetable stock*
			(canned is fine)
Bring to boil; pour over fish.			
Bake in **preheated** 375° oven.			

To complete recipe, you will need...	¹/₄	**cup**	*fresh basil,* chopped
	4	**tablespoons**	*butter,* broken into pieces

Bake halibut until done, approximately 10 to 15 minutes. Remove fish and keep warm. Boil *vegetable mixture* if needed until most of the liquid is gone. Add *chopped basil* and stir in *butter*. Serve vegetable mixture over fish.

Any firm fish can be substituted here (Chilean sea bass, salmon, etc.) And, of course, you can also vary the vegetable mixture to your taste!

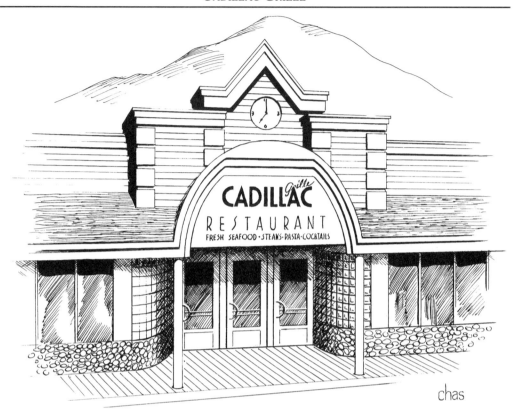

chas

On the west side of Jackson's town square, the Cadillac Grille offers a unique experience for the traveler and resident alike. The moment guests walk through the glass and mahogany doors, they are transported into another era by the award winning 1940s art deco atmosphere. Surrounded by buildings of a predominately western theme, the Cadillac makes a statement with its interior design. While its dining room is contemporary with white table linens and Philip Stark inspired furnishings, the lounge has more of an art deco influence, with salmon rose marble and glass block.

The Cadillac offers an eclectic menu which has been honed over the years by chef-owner Susan Marino. Executive chef David Belcher brings new dimensions to the Cadillac's cuisine by way of San Francisco and Miami. Their staff will please any palette with their mouth-watering entrees, presented in an exceptionally artful and colorful manner. They continue to feature Black Anus steaks, fresh seafood, wild game, imported pastas and pizza baked in a wood fired oven imported from Italy.

In addition to its dining room and outdoor patio, patrons can dine perched atop period stools at the California red granite bar; or if they choose, they can escape the bar bustling with high energy by hiding out in any of the deep retire-styled booths. In the bar, from lunch time straight through the dinner hour, patrons can choose to dine off the regular menu or select a juicy half-pound hamburger from the adjoining Billy's Burger diner.

The Cadillac Grille and staff offer a dining experience to fit any mood. Join them for an afternoon or evening you won't forget!

MENU FOR FOUR

Cheese-Onion Quiche Appetizer

recommended wine - big flavored, fruity chardonnay
Kenwood Yulupa Chardonnay

Frisee Salad with Maple-Balsamic Vinaigrette

Garlic-Peppercorn Encrusted Buffalo New York Strips with Wild Mushroom Sauce

recommended wine - lightly spiced zinfandel with lots of berry and fruit
Rancho Zabaco "Dancing Bull" Zinfandel

Creamy Polenta

Zabaglione with Huckleberries

recommended wine - very rich dessert wine with blackberry and blueberry
Essencia

Chef Suzanne Marino

Wine pairings by The Wine Loft

CHEESE-ONION QUICHE APPETIZERS

These are delicious served room temperature and enjoyed with a rich chardonnay.

For this recipe, you will need...			**pie crust dough,** your favorite recipe*
In saucepan, combine...	4	tablespoons	**butter**
	2	large	**white onions,** minced
Simmer over low heat for 1 hour.			

Add and cook for 3 minutes...	2	large	**tomatoes,** seeded, diced
	1	teaspoon	**basil**
Remove from heat.			

In mixing bowl, toss together...	5	ounces	**swiss cheese,** grated
	5	ounces	**gruyere,** grated
	2	tablespoons	**flour**
Stir ²/₃ of this mixture into onion/tomato mixture.			

In another bowl, mix together...	2	large	**eggs**
	³/₄	cup	**heavy cream**

Roll pie dough out into a rectangle to fit into a baking sheet. Sprinkle the remaining 1/3 cheese mixture over the top of pie dough. Pour the onion/tomato/cheese mixture on top. Finally, pour the egg/cream mixture on top. bake in a **preheated** 350° oven for 25-35 minutes, until custard is set and crust is slightly golden. Allow to cool, then cut into fun shapes...triangles, crazy rectangles, diamonds, etc. Serve room temperature.

FRISEE SALAD with
MAPLE BALSAMIC VINAIGRETTE

Serves 4

Frisee is of the endive family. It's taste is light and tart, not bitter, and makes a wonderful salad when combined with this vinaigrette.

In salad bowl, combine...	1	pound	*Frisee leaves,* broken into pieces
	1/2	cup	*walnuts,* toasted, chopped
	1/2	cup	*blue cheese,* crumbled

In salad bowl, place Frisse and toss with enough Maple-Balsamic Vinaigrette to lightly coat leaves. Portion onto salad plates and garnish each salad with *toasted walnuts* and *blue cheese crumbles.*

Maple Balsamic Vinaigrette

In mixing bowl, whisk together...	1/2	cup	*pure maple syrup*
	1/2	cup	*balsamic vinegar*
	1/4	cup	*rice wine vinegar*
	2	cloves	*garlic,* minced
	1	pinch	*dry mustard*
	1	pinch	*thyme*
While whisking, slowly add...	1 1/2	cup	*extra virgin olive oil*

Whisk vinaigrette again before dressing salad if it has separated before using.

GARLIC-PEPPERCORN ENCRUSTED BUFFALO NEW YORK STRIPS with WILD MUSHROOM SAUCE

Serves 4

Buffalo will cook faster than regular beef because it lacks the fat content. Be prepared to sit down and eat when you put the steaks on the grill! For the optimum texture and flavor, buffalo is best served rare to medium rare.

For this recipe, you will need...

4	8 oz	*buffalo New York strips**
1/2	cup	*olive oil*
3	tablespoons	*garlic,* minced

Mix olive oil and garlic together. Rub all over buffalo steaks.

Mix together...

2	tablespoons	*black peppercorns*
2	tablespoons	*white peppercorns*
2	tablespoons	*red peppercorns*

Crush in spice grinder or *clean* coffee grinder. Combine with...

1	tablespoon	*green peppercorns,* crushed with side of knife

Spread peppercorns evenly over a large plate. Roll buffalo steaks, just on the sides, through peppercorns, coating sides but not on the top or bottom of steak. Cook over a very hot grill until done. Be sure not to over cook! Remember...rare to medium rare at most. Serve steaks with Wild Mushroom Sauce.

*Available at Jackson Hole Buffalo Meat Co. (see Participating Restaurants Index, page v).

Wild Mushroom Sauce

Go to your local gourmet market and purchase 2 pounds of the best assortment of mushrooms you can find. Grocers traditionally have portabello, shitake, ceps, and domestic varieties. If you are able to find chanterelles or truffles, they add a robust finish to the sauce. If you aren't able to find any fresh mushrooms other than domestic, purchase a dried forest mushroom mixture, or any assortment of the dried mushrooms mentioned above, and follow the directions for rehydration.

Be sure to wash all mushrooms very well to remove any grit or dirt from them.

In large sauté pan, over medium heat, combine...	2-4	tablespoons	*olive oil*
	2	pounds	*fresh assorted wild mushrooms,* sliced
		[OR]	
	1	pound	*dried mushrooms,* rehydrated, sliced
	4	large cloves	*garlic,* minced
			salt and pepper to taste
Cook, stirring constantly, for 2-3 minutes			

Turn heat to low and add...	1	cup	*red wine* (merlot!)
Simmer briefly.			
Stir in...	4	leaves	*basil,* minced
	1	sprig	*thyme,* leaves only, minced
	$^{1}/_{2}$	cup	*veal demi glace**
Cook long enough to heat through. Remove from heat and add...	1	tablespoon	*butter*

Stir until butter is broken down and adds a creamy consistency.

*Available in culinary stores/catalogs; see index for recipe or quick substitutions.

CREAMY POLENTA

This dish is best when prepared just before sitting down to eat.

In saucepan, combine...	3	cups	*milk*
	1¹/₂	tablespoons	*sea salt*
	3	tablespoons	*unsalted butter*
Bring to a boil; cook for 2 minutes. Remove from heat and, while whisking, add...	1	cup	*polenta* (Italian style grain cornmeal)

Place mixture back onto low heat and simmer, constantly beating with a wooden spoon until mixture thickens and pulls away from the side of the pan.

| While stirring, add... | ¹/₂ | cup | *mascarpone cheese* |
| | 1 | tablespoon | *heavy cream* |

Continue stirring until a creamy consistency is achieved. Add more *warm milk* if necessary.

ZABAGLIONE with HUCKLEBERRIES

A wonderful Italian dessert, served Wyoming style with wild huckleberries. We use champagne in our Zabaglione; however, marsala wine is traditionally used.

This is also best when made just prior to serving. With everything ready, it only takes about 5 minutes to complete.

For this recipe, you will need...	2	cups	*huckleberries**
	4	each	*Itallian Pizzells or biscotti*
			fresh mint (garnish)

| In medium size bowl, whisk together... | 6 | | *egg yolks* |
| | 1¹/₃ | cups | *heavy cream* |

In saucepan, combine...	2²/₃	cups	*half and half*
	³/₄	cup	*sugar*

Bring to a simmer, stirring
to dissolve sugar. Remove
from heat.

Slowly add, while whisking, 1/2 cup of this mixture to egg yolk mixture. Then slowly add, while whisking, all of egg yolk mixture to hot half and half mixture. Now place over medium heat and stir constantly until the mixture begins to thicken and coats the back of a spoon (approximately 5 minutes).

Slowly, stir in...	¹/₂	cup	*champagne*
			(room temperature)

Strain custard through a fine sieve or cheese cloth into a bowl. Serve immediately if possible. If not, cover with plastic wrap, (plastic wrap directly on top of custard). Set aside at room temperature.

To serve, spoon zabaglione into beautiful stem glasses of choice or pretty glass dessert cups; top with ¹/₃ to ¹/₂ cup of fresh huckleberries (or frozen and thawed huckleberries). Garnish with fresh mint sprig. Serve with pizzell or biscotti cookies.

Available at Huckleberry Mountain (see Participating Restaurants Index, page v).

MENU FOR SIX

Roma Tomato and Goat Cheese Salad

Steamed Prince Edward Island Mussels

recommended wine ⁓ dry, creamy, very smooth sauvignon blanc
Groth Sauvignon Blanc

Chianti Braised Lamb Shank

recommended wine ⁓ medium-bodied, very fruitful merlot with a light, smooth finish
Canoe Ridge Merlot

Chocolate-Espresso Pate

recommended wine ⁓ medium-bodied port with a thick blackberry-plum palate
Graham's Six Grapes Port

Chef David Belcher

Wine pairings by The Wine Loft

ROMA TOMATO and GOAT CHEESE SALAD

Serves 4

Slice, medium thick...	4	ripe/plump	*roma tomatoes,* room temperature
Slice as thin as possible without breaking apart...	1	8 oz. tube	*goat cheese,* chilled (easier to slice cold)

On salad plates, arrange slices of tomato and goat cheese alternately.

Drizzle with...		*extra virgin olive oil*
Sprinkle with...	1	small bunch	*fresh basil,* chiffonade* *salt* *black pepper* finely ground

Serve room temperature.

*Chiffonade refers to a technique of slicing or shredding vegetables. In the case of basil; pile up several basil leaves, gently roll them up lengthwise, and slice very thinly with sharp knife. This technique prevents the edges of the basil from turning black.

STEAMED PRINCE EDWARD ISLAND MUSSELS

Serves 4

Warm large sauté pan over medium heat and add...	2	tablespoons	*olive oil*
	1	clove	*garlic,* minced
	24		*Prince Edward Island Mussels*
Cook until garlic is golden brown. Add...	1½	cups	*dry white wine*

Cover and cook for 5 minutes until all mussels have opened. Divide mussels among four serving dishes.

Place sauté pan with wine back
over medium heat and
swirl in... $^1/_4$ **cup**   *butter,* diced small

Pour wine butter over mussels. Serve.

CHIANTI BRAISED LAMB SHANK   Serves 4

Dredge in flour seasoned with
salt and pepper...   4   *lamb shanks*

In hot skillet, heat...   2   **tablespoons**   *olive oil*

Add shanks to skillet and sear until golden brown on all sides. Remove from pan. Set aside until needed.

In same pan, over medium
heat, sauté...   1   **large**   *onion,* diced medium
                                             4   **stalks**   *celery,* diced medium
                                             3   **medium**   *carrots,* diced medium
Sauté until union is translucent.

Add...   2   **cloves**   *garlic,* minced
Sauté until golden brown.

Add...   1   **cup**   *tomatoes* (canned)
                                                                          chopped
                                             1   **cup**   *chianti*
                                             4   **sprigs**   *fresh thyme*
                                             2   **whole**   *bay leaves*
                                                                      salt and pepper
                                                                         to taste
Cook to reduce by half.

| Add and bring to a boil... | 4 | cups | *chicken stock** |

Place lamb shanks in roasting pan. Pour vegetables and broth over shanks and cover with foil. Bake in **preheated** 350° oven for about $1^1/_2$ hours, until meat is very tender. Serve with mashed potatoes or creamy polenta (see recipe on previous page of Cadillac recipes).

*Homemade is best (see index for recipe); or good quality chicken base with water, or canned broth.

CHOCOLATE-ESPRESSO PATÉ

In bowl, combine...	1	cup	*espresso coffee*
	10	broken up	*Famous Chocolate Wafer Cookies**
Soak cookies in espresso.			

| Press through a fine sieve into mixing bowl... | 9 | | *egg yolks,* hard cooked |

Add...	1 $^1/_2$	cups	*unsalted butter*
			room temperature
Blend with electric mixer until smooth.			

Add...	12	ounces	*semi-sweet chocolate*
			melted
	$^1/_2$	cup	*cocoa*
	$^3/_4$	cup	*chocolate fudge topping* (canned)
	2	tablespoons	*vanilla extract*
	2	tablespoons	*brandy*
	2	tablespoons	*amaretto*
Beat until light and fluffy, about 10 minutes.			

Stir in...   6 ¹/₂   ounces   *semi-sweet chocolate*
                                                        shaved

Grease a 9" x 5" loaf pan with oil, then line pan with plastic wrap (oiled sides holds plastic in place nicely while spreading chocolate mixture in pan). Spread a third of chocolate mixture into bottom of loaf pan. Cover with half of the soaked cookies; follow with another layer of chocolate mixture, then remaining cookies; and a final layer of chocolate mixture. Refrigerate for 3 to 4 hours or longer.

To serve, remove from freezer a few minutes before serving. Invert pan onto a tray or plate. Slice loaf into ¹/₂" thick slices. Pour pools of **raspberry puree** (or liberally drizzle in diagonal pattern) on small plates. Place slice of pate on top.

chas

For more than 35 years the Calico has been a locals' favorite for great pizza, pasta and salads, as well as a gathering place for friends to meet after work or play. With it's beautiful sweeping lawns, flowering gardens and large deck, it is a great place for families to congregate. With outdoor games and toys available for improptu games of catch, frisbee, and tag, kids have always been encouraged to play and enjoy themselves while parents relax.

In 1995, Jeff Davies became the proud new owner of Calico. Still a great place to find gourmet pizza, Calico's dinner menu has greatly expanded to include creative and traditional pastas, fresh seafood, decadent desserts and great wines. With its beautifully redesigned, enlarged dining room, and expanded deck, it is more alive than ever with the sounds of people enjoying great food and camaraderie in comfortable surroundings.

With herbs, vegetables and greens growing in its garden, and a huge green lawn for kids to romp on, the Calico is still a locals' favorite. Visitors also, return year after year to the friendly beckoning of Calico Italian Restaurant and Bar.

MENU FOR SIX

Tomato Bruschetta

recommended wine - very light, crisp, smooth pinot gris
Zenato Pinot Grigio

Hearts of Palm Salad

recommended wine - sauvignon blanc with light fruit flavors and creamy vanilla finish
Silverado Sauvignon Blanc

Grilled Sea Bass in Jade Sauce

recommended wine - riesling with balance of dryness and light berry flavor
Trimbach Riesling

Roasted Red Pepper Rice

Wyoming Marionberry Cobbler

recommended wine - dessert wine rich with honey and spice
Bonny Doon Muscat

Wine pairings by The Wine Loft

TOMATO BRUSCHETTA
Serves 6

For this recipe, you will need...

1	loaf	*French baguette*
$^1/_2$	cup	*extra virgin olive oil*

Slice bread into approximately 24 slices, each about $^1/_3$" thick. Place on baking sheet and drizzle with *olive oil*. Bake in **preheated** 375° oven until toasted light brown. Remove and cool.

In mixing bowl, combine...

7	ripe	*roma tomatoes,* seeded, diced into $^1/_4$" inch pieces
3	cloves	*garlic,* finely minced
1	whole	*shallot,* finely minced
8	large	*basil leaves,* finely chopped
4	ounces	*fresh mozzarella,* cut into small pieces

Toss with...

$^1/_2$	cup	*extra virgin olive oil*
		salt to taste
		freshly cracked pepper to taste

To serve, arrange toasts on a platter and place a dollop of bruschetta mixture on each.

HEARTS OF PALM SALAD

In large salad bowl, place...	1	pound	*spring greens*

Toss greens with ³/₄ of **Vinaigrette**. Distribute greens on six salad plates.

In mixing bowl, combine...	2	cups	*artichoke hearts,* quartered
	2	cups	*hearts of palm,* sliced

Toss with remainder of **Vinaigrette**; place portion of mixture on each serving of greens.

Garnish each salad with portion of...	2	ripe	*roma tomatoes,* seeded, chopped
	1	small	*red onion,* thinly sliced
			parmesan cheese, freshly shredded

Vinaigrette

In mixing bowl, combine...	¹/₃	cup	*red wine vinegar*
	1	tablespoon	*sugar*
	1¹/₂	teaspoons	*dijon mustard*
	1¹/₂	teaspoons	*oregano*
	1¹/₂	teaspoons	*basil*
	1	teaspoon	*salt*
	1	teaspoon	*black pepper*

Whisking continuously, slowly add...	1	cup	*canola oil*

GRILLED CHILEAN SEA BASS in JADE SAUCE   Serves 6

For this recipe, you will need...	6	5 oz. pieces	*Chilean Sea Bass*
	12	large	*fresh basil leaves*
			olive oil
			salt and pepper

Rub sea bass with *olive oil,* sprinkle with *salt and pepper.* For fish pieces 1" thick, cook on hot grill approximately 2 minutes per side.

To serve, place a mound of **Roasted Red Pepper Rice** into center of each plate; ladle about $1/4$ cup of **Jade Sauce** around rice. Place grilled sea bass on top of rice and garnish with fried *basil.* [Fry basil leaves in very hot oil for approximately 20 seconds.]

Jade Sauce

For this recipe, you will need...	1	large bunch	*fresh cilantro*
			(must yield 1 cup packed leaves)

Rinse, pat dry, remove stems.

In food processor, combine cilantro leaves with...	$1/4$	cup	*rice wine vinegar*
	1	tablespoon	*orange juice*
	$1/2$	tablespoon	*honey*
	2	teaspoons	*ginger,* minced
	1	teaspoon	*garlic,* minced
	1	teaspoon	*salt*

Chop until cilantro is minced.

With machine running, slowly add...	$1/2$	cup	*grape seed oil*
	$1/2$	tablespoon	*sesame oil*

Once emulsion forms, let processor run a minute longer to insure infusion of cilantro and color. Set aside at room temperature until ready to use.

ROASTED RED PEPPER RICE   Serves 6-8

Cook according to package instructions...	3	cups	*basmati rice*

Over open flame, roast until charred...	2	whole	*red bell peppers*
Place in paper bag for 15 minutes. Remove from bag. Peel, seed and julienne peppers.			

In sauté pan, heat...	$^1/_2$	cup	*canola oil*
Add...	3	baby	*bok choy,* cut into $^1/_4$" slices
Stir-fry for 2 minutes.			

Stir in...	*red pepper julienne* *cooked rice* *salt and pepper* *to taste*

Serve with Grilled Chilean Sea Bass.

WYOMING MARIONBERRY COBBLER   Serves 6

In stainless steel saucepan, combine...	$^1/_3$	cup	*sugar*
	$^1/_3$	cup	*water*
	$1^1/_2$	ounces	*cornstarch*
	1	teaspoon	*vanilla*
Stir over medium heat until very thick and beginning to bubble.			

| Remove from heat and add... | 1¹/₂ | pounds | *marionberries* |

Stir to combine and heat.

Portion out into six 8 oz. ramekins. Sprinkle liberally with **Topping**, place on baking sheet and bake in **preheated** 275° oven for 30 minutes. Serve warm with scoop of vanilla ice cream.

<u>Topping</u>

In mixer bowl, combine...	3	ounces	*oats*
	7	ounces	*flour*
	10	ounces	*brown sugar*
	1¹/₂	teaspoon	*cinnamon*

| With mixer running, add... | ¹/₃ | pound | *butter,* melted |

To store, place in covered container in refrigerator

chas

High atop the East Gros Ventre Butte in Jackson Hole, the Granary Restaurant at Spring Creek Ranch offers magnificent views of the Grand Tetons and the valley below, through its towering cathedral windows. In such an awe-inspiring ambiance, guests enjoy breakfast, lunch and dinner, in addition to a tantalizing Sunday brunch.

In addition to it's fine restaurant, Spring Creek Ranch provides condominiums and a hotel with swimming pool, jacuzzi, tennis courts, horseback riding, cross country ski touring, and much more for its guests and the residents of Jackson.

Chef Kevin Gries uses many local and regional ingredients to create a delicious dining experience. His menu offers guests the pleasure of tasting many different game entrees and appetizers, uniquely prepared.

MENU FOR FOUR

Wild Huckleberry and Pecan Stuffed Quail with Sweet Potato Cakes

recommended wine - pinot gris with balance of dryness and light berry
Elk Cove Pinot Gris

SCR Spinach Salad with Grilled Portabello Dressing

recommended wine - chardonnay with lots of fruit flavor - citrus, pear, pineapple
Sonoma-Cutrer Chardonnay

Roast Tenderloin of Antelope with Roast Garlic Jus and Black Peppercorn Lingonberry Jam

recommended wine - very dry, full-bodied red bordeaux
Chateau Meyney Saint Emilion

Wild Rice Barley Pilaf

Swiss Chard

Huckleberry Creme Caramel

recommended wine - rich, sweet dessert wine bursting with flavor
Royal Tokaji

Chef Kevin Gries
Wine pairings by The Wine Loft

WILD HUCKLEBERRY and PECAN STUFFED QUAIL with SWEET POTATO CAKES

Serves 4

At fine poultry/meat markets, a butcher will be happy to debone your quails for you.

| For this recipe, you will need... | 4 | 4 ounce | *quail breasts,* boneless |
| | 2 | cups | *wild rice,* cooked |

In sauté pan, over medium flame, heat...	2	tablespoons	*butter*
	1	teaspoon	*shallots,* minced
	1	teaspoon	*garlic,* minced

Add...			*cooked rice*
	1/4	cup	*huckleberries*
	1	tablespoon	*pecans,* finely chopped
	1	teaspoon	*fresh rosemary,* chopped
	1	teaspoon	*fresh thyme,* chopped
	2	tablespoons	*vegetable broth*
			salt and pepper to taste

Cook two minutes to emulsify. Cool down.

| Add... | 3/4 | cup | *ricotta cheese* |

Stuff cavity of quail with mixture. Roast in **preheated** 350° oven for approximately 12-15 minutes, depending on size of quail. Serve with Sweet Potato Cake and Herbed Balsamic Emulsion.

Sweet Potato Cakes

| In **preheated** 350° oven, roast for 50 minutes... | 2 | whole | *sweet potatoes* |

Let cool, peel and mash.

Place mashed sweet potatoes in
mixer and add...

1	whole	*egg*
1	tablespoon	*pure maple syrup*
1	pinch	*nutmeg*
1	pinch	*black pepper*

Mix well. Form into 3" cakes,
$1/2$" thick. Dredge in...

$1/2$	cup	*flour*

In sauté pan, over medium flame
heat...

2	tablespoons	*olive oil*

Add sweet potato cakes and sauté until golden brown/orange, about 2 minutes on each side. Drain on paper towel. Keep warm or reheat in **preheated** 350° oven for 5 minutes before serving. Serve with Sweet Potato Cakes and Herbed Balsamic Emulsion.

Herbed Balsamic Emulsion

In blender or food processor,
combine...

$1/4$	cup	*aged balsamic vinegar*
1	tablespoon	*garlic,* minced
1	tablespoon	*shallots,* chopped
1	tablespoon	*fresh thyme,* leaves only
1	tablespoon	*whole grain mustard*

With machine running, slowly
add...

$3/4$	cup	*extra virgin olive oil*

Then add...

2	tablespoons	*honey*

Stir in by hand...

1	tablespoon	*fresh basil,* julienned

SCR SPINACH SALAD
with GRILLED PORTABELLO DRESSING   Serves 4

For you portabello mushroom lovers, here's a salad well worth the extra effort and preparation....you'll love it! What a great combination of flavors and texture!

For this recipe, you will need...	1	pound	**baby spinach,** cleaned, stems removed
Keep chilled until use.			

Prepare the following...	1	whole	**granny smith apple,*** peeled, seeded, julienned
	1	bulb	**fennel,** shaved thinly
	6	ounces	**Proscuitto di Parma,** julienned
	6	ounces	**goat cheese,** crumbled

In large salad bowl, toss spinach and all ingredients with Grilled Portabello Dressing and freshly cracked black pepper.

*If preparing ahead, dip apple slices in a lemon water bath to prevent them from turning brown.

Grilled Portabello Dressing

Rub with **olive oil** and salt and pepper; grill...	2	large	**portabello mushrooms***
Cool down and chop up.			

In blender or food processor, puree...	$1/4$	cup	*cider vinegar*
	$3/4$	cup	*balsamic vinegar*
	$1/4$	cup	*shallots,* minced
	2	tablespoons	*dijon mustard*
	1	tablespoon	*garlic,* crushed
	2	teaspoons	*black peppercorns*
	1	teaspoon	*kosher salt*

Slowly add to emulsify...	3	cups	*extra virgin olive oil*
Finish with adding...	1	tablespoon	*fresh thyme*
	1	tablespoon	*fresh basil*

*If you don't have a BBQ grill, a great trick to bring out that smoky, earthy taste of grilled portabellos is to cook them right on the electric burner on your stovetop!

ROAST TENDERLOIN OF ANTELOPE with ROAST GARLIC JUS and BLACK PEPPERCORN LINGONBERRY JAM   Serves 4

In Jackson Hole, many people still hunt their own game. If you can't do that, most good butchers can supply you with antelope when ordered ahead.

Start preparation a day ahead, as the antelope needs to marinate at least 12 hours, and even better, up to 24 hours. This is one of the more involved recipes in this book, but well worth the effort. What a way to impress your guests! Drink some wine....have fun spending the afternoon creating in the kitchen!

Cut into 8 ounce portions...	2	pounds	*antelope tenderloin*
In mixing bowl, combine...	1/4	cup	*canola oil*
	1	whole	*shallot,* minced
(marinade)	1	tablespoon	*juniper berries,* crushed*
	2	teaspoons	*black peppercorns,* crushed*
	1	pinch	*nutmeg*
	1	pinch	*cloves*

Place antelope portions in marinade, covered, for 12 to 24 hours. Grill over high heat to sear quickly on all sides (or sear in very hot skillet); place in **preheated** 450° oven for 7 to 8 minutes to finish. Chef Kevin Gries suggests medium rare for best taste and texture. To serve, slice diagonally into equal portions, allowing three medallions each.

For a beautiful presentation, Kevin suggests placing the three medallions on each plate in the positions of 4, 8 and 12 on a clock. Place portion of **Wild Rice Barley Pilaf** in the center of the plate, with the **Swiss Chard** on top. Ladle the **Roast Garlic Jus** onto the plate around the medallions and rice pilaf. Place three small dollops of the Bla**ck Pepper Lingonberry Jam**, one dollop between each medallion.

A crowning touch for those zealous chefs out there....Deep fry long, thin julienne of *sweet potato* and pile it high on top of the swiss chard. Voila!

*A **clean** coffee grinder works well for crushing spices.*

Roast Garlic Jus

Have plenty of merlot wine on hand to create this jus!

In heavy saucepan, combine...	2	tablespoons	*canola oil*
	1	small	*carrot,* finely chopped
(mire poix)	1	small	*celery rib,* finely chopped
	1	large	*red onion,* minced
	15	cloves	*garlic,* minced
Cook over medium heat until golden brown (almost caramelized). Add...	2	tablespoons	*tomato paste*
Continue cooking until caramelized.			

Add...	3	sprigs	*fresh rosemary*
	3	whole	*bay leaves*
	1	tablespoon	*black peppercorns*
	3	cups	*merlot wine*
Reduce by 75% and add...	3	add'l cups	*merlot*
Reduce by 50% and add...	3	last cups	*merlot*
	2	cups	*veal or beef stock**
Reduce by about 25%, until it coats the back of a spoon.			

Place reduction in blender or food processor and puree. Strain through a fine chinois (china cap) or fine sieve. Season to taste with salt and pepper. Serve.

*Homemade is best (see index for recipe); or use a good quality canned consommé.

Black Peppercorn Lingonberry Jam

Combine...	1/2	cup	*lingonberry jam*
	1	tablespoon	*black peppercorns,* freshly cracked
	1	tablespoon	*fresh cilantro,* julienned
Mix well and refrigerate.			

WILD RICE BARLEY PILAF   Serves 4

The wild rice and barley can be cooked ahead and refrigerated if you like until needed to finish recipe.

In small saucepan, bring to boil...	1	cup	*water*
	1/2	cup	*barley,* rinsed well
Simmer over low heat, covered, until liquid is gone, about 40 minutes. Toss with fork.			

In another saucepan, bring to boil...	2	cups	*water*
	1	cup	*wild rice,* rinsed well
Simmer over low heat until liquid is gone, about 40 minutes. Toss with fork.			

In sauté pan, over medium flame, heat...	3	tablespoons	*butter*
	1	tablespoon	*shallots,* minced
Stir in...			*cooked rice*
			cooked barley
	1	sprig	*fresh rosemary,* leaves only finely chopped

| Stir in... | 1/4 | cup | *merlot wine* |

Continue stirring to a risotto
consistency and texture.

Season to taste with *salt and pepper*. Serve.

SWISS CHARD

Serves 4

In saucepan, heat...	2	tablespoons	*butter*
	1	tablespoon	*shallots,* minced
Add...	1	tablespoon	*garlic,* minced
	1	pound	*swiss chard*

Saute for one minute.

| Deglaze with... | 1/4 | cup | *dry white wine* |

Cook over medium heat, stirring occasionally, for about 3 minutes. Season to taste with
salt and pepper. Serve.

HUCKLEBERRY CREME CARAMEL

Serves 4

Be sure to have your custard ramekins ready for when your sugar has caramelized.

| For this recipe, you will need... | 4 | tablespoons | *huckleberries** |

| In heavy skillet, over medium high heat, combine... | 1 | cup | *sugar* |
| | ¼ | cup | *water* |

Stir until like a wet sand.

Cook , stirring occasionally until sugar mixture turns to caramel. Immediately pour equal portions of the caramel into four 6 ounce oven safe ramekins. Set aside.

| In saucepan combine... | 2 | cups | *milk* |
| | 2 | teaspoons | *vanilla*** |

Bring milk to a scald.

| In a mixer or bowl, beat until fluffy... | 6 | whole | *eggs* |
| | ½ cup + 2 | tablespoons | *white sugar* |

| Stirring rapidly, slowly add... | ¼ | cup | *scalded milk* |

Still stirring, slowly add the rest of the milk to finish custard.

Pour custard over the caramel in the ramekins. Sprinkle one tablespoon of *huckleberries* into each custard. Bake custards in water bath in **preheated** 300° oven for 20- 30 minutes, or until set. [To test, use a small paring knife stuck into middle of custard; it should come out clean.]

*Available at Huckleberry Mountain (see Participating Restaurants Index, page v).

**Or use one whole vanilla bean and discard after scalding milk.

chas

There is something very special about dining at Jenny Lake Lodge, in the heart of Grand Teton National Park. A small, rustically elegant retreat which had its beginnings in the 1920s, it sits quietly tucked against fragrant pines in the shadow of the Grand Teton. Those fortunate enough to stay at this marvelous lodge will enjoy every meal at Jenny Lake Dining Room. You will also find many Jackson residents enjoying the serenity of dining, while the sun is setting, or leisurely enjoying the Lodge's famous Sunday brunch.

Guests at the Lodge are treated to western style historic cabins beautifully appointed with down comforters and hand made quilts. No television is necessary, thank you! The view of the Tetons from the main lodge is spectacular, with hiking trails and three lakes within easy walking distance. A boat ride across Jenny Lake takes you to within a quarter mile of the beautiful Hidden Falls. Bicycling and horseback riding are available also.

Executive Chef Joseph Santangini sets the menu and creates the recipes for the Jenny Lake Dining Room. With many awards to his credit, including "1997 Chef of the Year" presented by the Golden Isles Chefs Association of the American Culinary Federation, he's delighted to express his culinary talents for the benefit and pleasure of his guests.

MENU FOR FOUR

Caesar Salad

Salmon Quenelles with Lobster Sauce

recommended wine ~ buttery California chardonnay with lots of oak
ZD Chardonnay

Smoked Beef Tenderloin

recommended wine ~ big cabernet with bold berry flavors
Joseph Phelps Cabernet Sauvignon

Chocolate Bourbon Pecan Torte

recommended wine ~ dessert wine with berry
Bonny Doon Framboise

Chef Joseph Santangini

Wine pairings by The Wine Loft

CAESAR SALAD
Serves 4

For this recipe, you will need...	1 ½	cups	*croutons*
Wash, drain well and tear into bite-size pieces...	1-2	heads	*romaine*

It is most important when making a caesar salad that the romaine is <u>cold</u> and <u>crisp</u> before mixing with the dressing. Place prepared romaine into a cloth bag and chill in refrigerator 2 hours before serving.

Just before serving, toss romaine with desired amount of *croutons* and about 1 cup of **Caesar Dressing**. You can always add more dressing if you like your caesar 'wetter.'

Caesar Dressing

Be sure to make the dressing several hours ahead so it can chill in the refrigerator.

In food processor, combine...	³/₄	cup	*red wine vinegar*
	1	tablespoon	*garlic*
	1	ounce	*anchovies*
	2	teaspoons	*worcestershire*
	2	tablespoons	*fresh lemon juice*
	2	tablespoons	*parmesan cheese*
	½	teaspoon	*kosher salt*
	1	teaspoon	*white peppercorns,* cracked
	1	pinch	*sugar*
With machine running, add...	1½	cups	*vegetable oil*
	³/₄	cup	*olive oil*

Adjust seasonings. Chill and store in covered container until ready to use.

SALMON QUENELLES with LOBSTER SAUCE
Serves 4

Always use only the freshest salmon for this recipe; never use frozen fish. Classically made with pike in France, quenelles of sole are delicious as well.

Prepared and poached with care, these will melt in your mouth!

In saucepan, combine...	3$^1/_4$	ounces	*white wine* (chablis)
	1$^1/_4$	ounces	*shallots,* minced
Reduce until liquid is almost gone.			

In large food processor, grind up...	1$^1/_4$	pounds	*fresh salmon,* skinned
Add...			*shallot-wine reduction*
	1$^5/_8$	cups	*heavy cream*
	6$^5/_8$	ounces	*egg whites*
	3	ounces	*lobster base**
	6	tablespoons	*brandy*
	$^3/_4$	whole	*lemon,* juice only
Puree to a fine smooth consistency.			

Form the quenelle mixture into small 'dumplings' using two spoons. Put one spoon in a bowl of hot water. Using the other spoon, gently scoop out enough of the mixture to fill the spoon. Invert the hot, moist spoon over the filled spoon to shape the quenelle. Don't press hard. You are merely shaping the quenelle into an egg shape. Place your quenelles, one by one into a buttered pan. Allow space for expansion between all quenelles. The quenelles can be prepared to this point an hour or two ahead. Be sure to store them, tightly covered (but plastic not touching them), in the refrigerator until ready to poach.

To poach the quenelles, carefully pour water (or stock) which has just come to a boil, into the pan from the sides, so as not to disturb the quenelles. The water should come half way up the quenelles. Over low heat, simmer gently for 10 minutes (water/stock should be barely quivering. As the quenelles cook, they will become light and rise and turn over. The weight of the uncooked portion will partially submerge them. They are done when they once again float. Serve immediately with Lobster Sauce.

*Available in gourmand section of fine grocers, culinary stores or catalogs.

Lobster Sauce

In heavy saucepan, combine and
    reduce by two thirds...

	3	cups	*lobster stock**
	2	cups	*dry white wine*
	{ 1		*leek,* white part only
(bouquet garni)	{ 3	sprigs	*fresh thyme*
	{ 1	whole	*bay leaf*

To make a bouquet garni, using white part only, cut leek in half and pull out the center; leaving about 4 layers of leek. In the middle of the leek, place the fresh thyme and bay leaf. Place the other half of the leek on top of the filled leek; tie the leek with butcher's twine. Bouquet garni!

Add...	2	quarts	*heavy cream*

    Let reduce to desired consistency.

    Season with...   *salt and white pepper to taste*

If made with lobster base, be careful with the amount of salt to you add to recipe.

SMOKED BEEF TENDERLOIN
Serves 4

This would be terrific served with garlic or horseradish mashed potatoes.

For this recipe, you will need...	3	pounds	*beef tenderloin*
			salt
			black pepper, freshly cracked
			garlic powder
			rosemary
			hickory chips
			butter

Strip whole tenderloin of all fat, gristle and silverskin. Season well with salt, pepper, garlic and rosemary. Place in smoker with *hickory chips,* at low temperature setting, for 3 hours.

Remove tenderloin from smoker and place in roasting pan. Brush with *butter.* Roast in **preheated** 350° oven for about 20 minutes for rare (115° internal temperature); or 25-30 minutes for medium to well (125° to 130°). Allow beef to rest for 10 minutes before carving.

CHOCOLATE BOURBON PECAN TORTE   Makes Two

In saucepan, over low heat, melt together...	5	ounces	*butter*
	5	ounces	*dark chocolate*
In small bowl, mix together...	7 7/8	ounces	*white sugar*
	3 1/4	ounces	*cocoa powder*
Add to chocolate mixture.			
In another bowl, whip...	7/8	cup	*eggs*
Whip until frothy.			
Fold in...	1 3/4	ounces	*bourbon whiskey*
	5	ounces	*pecan halves*

Pour mix into 9" greased and papered cake pans. Bake in **preheated** 350° oven for approximately 55 minutes. Remove from oven and allow to cool. Pour Chocolate Glaze over cake. Allow chocolate to set up a little, then garnish sides with *additional pecan pieces.* Place a pecan half on each slice.

Chocolate Glaze

In saucepan, over low heat, melt together...	1/2	pound	*butter*
	1	pound	*chocolate,* broken into pieces
Be sure to keep temperature			

chas

Joe and Sylvia Diprisco have owned the Lame Duck Chinese Restaurant for the past 20 years. Not possessing any real practical or professional training in oriental cooking was cause for a rocky start. By employing the services of Florence Lin, a well-known teacher and cookbook author, they were able to bridge the rough spots.

A trip to Hong Kong for several weeks of instruction in a Chinese cooking school (with interpreter!) gave Joe the expertise he needed to create a menu of authenticity with a wide assortment of dishes, including some Chinese, Hunan, and Szechwan. Another trip, to Tahiti, was responsible for a tropical influence to the Lame Duck's atmosphere and the introduction of tropical drinks.

Three of the most popular features of the restaurant are their private tea rooms for parties, the full bar featuring their world famous Super Mai Tai, and sushi, all of which illustrates Joe's willingness to borrow from any kind of cuisine he likes!

Thus, when you try these recipes or come to Jackson, you'll know why we say, "Don't miss the Lame Duck difference!" This is truly a unique oriental restaurant.

MENU FOR FOUR

Calamari Tempura

recommended wine ~ medium dry sake
Momokawa Sake

Hot and Sour Soup

Smoked Salmon and Avocado Sushi Roll

recommended wine ~ medium dry German riesling
Schlink Haus Spatleses

Mussels in Black Bean Sauce

recommended wine ~ dry chardonnay with light fruit
Lindemans Padthaway Chardonnay

Moo-Phi Dragon

recommended wine ~ riesling with tropical fruit, pear and peach
Columbia Riesling

Thai Fried Rice

Chef Joe Diprisco

Wine pairings by The Wine Loft

CALAMARI TEMPURA   Serves 4

In bowl, beat until bubbly...	2		*egg yolks*
Stir in...	2	cups	*ice cold water*
Add...	2	cups	*flour*

Cut into strips...	8	ounces	*calamari steaks*

Dip strips into batter and
    deep fry in...   *soy bean oil,*
                heated to 350°

Fry to light golden color,
about 1-2 minutes.

Serve with your choice of dipping sauces.

HOT AND SOUR SOUP   Makes 2 Quarts

In large saucepan, combine and heat...	8	cups	*chicken stock*
	3	ounces	*red wine vinegar*
	2	tablespoons	*soy sauce*
	1	tablespoon	*Thai chili garlic paste**

Add and bring to a gentle boil...	3	whole	*shitake mushrooms,* sliced
	1	ounce	*lily flowers*,* soaked in hot water; sliced

In bowl, mix together...	1/2	cup	*water*
	1/4	cup	*cornstarch*

Slowly add to soup,
stirring constantly.

To complete recipe, you will need...	2	whole	*eggs,* whipped
	4	whole	*green onions,* sliced

Turn heat down and allow soup to clarify. With heat on low, slowly dribble in *whipped eggs* and allow to cook. Serve garnished with *green onions.*

*Available in specialty sections of grocers; or see Spice Merchant (Participating Restaurants Index, page v.)

SMOKED SALMON and AVOCADO SUSHI ROLL Serves 4

For this recipe, you will need...	1	pound	*smoked salmon,* sliced into strips
In bowl, combine...	$3/4$	cup	*rice,* uncooked
	$1/2$	cup	*brown sugar*
	3-4	pieces	*star anise**
In saucepan, combine...	$1^{1}/_2$	cups	*water*
	1	cup	*short grain white rice,* rinsed twice with cold water
(sushi rice)			
	1	teaspoon	*mirin vinegar*
Bring to boil, cover and simmer over low heat for 10-12 minutes.			
In small bowl, combine...	2	tablespoons	*rice wine vinegar*
	$3/4$	teaspoon	*sugar*
	$1/2$	teaspoon	*salt*
To complete recipe, you will need...	4	sheets	*nori wrappers**
	$1/2$		*avocado,* peeled, pitted, sliced
			soy sauce

> wasabi*
> pickled ginger*
> bamboo sushi roller*

One at a time, place a *nori wrapper* (with 1 $1/2$" trimmed off any side) on *bamboo roller* and cover with *sushi rice,* leaving 1" along one side uncovered. Lay a couple strips of smoked salmon across the width of rice-covered nori wrapper. Place a strip of *avocado* down the middle of salmon. Using bamboo roller and starting with rice-covered edge of nori wrapper, roll seaweed towards bare edge of wrapper keeping the roll tight with even pressure; and along the way, enveloping the salmon and avocaco strips. When roll is completely wrapped to the bare edge, wet this edge with water or vinegar and press it against the roll to seal edge. Cut roll into 8-10 pieces and serve with *soy sauce, wasabi,* and *pickled ginger.*

Available in specialty sections of grocers; or see Spice Merchant (Participating Restaurants Index, page v).

MUSSELS IN BLACK BEAN SAUCE   Serves 4

To create this recipe for four servings, you will need a very large sauté pan or wok, or you can use two smaller pans and split the ingredients between them).

For this recipe, you will need...	24		**New Zealand Green Lip Mussels,** on half shell
	1	cup	**green onions,** sliced

In large wok or sauté pan, over medium high heat, combine...	$1/2$	**cup**	**soy bean oil,** heated
	4	**tablespoons**	**garlic,** minced
	4	**tablespoons**	**dry salted black beans*,** chopped
Sauté for 30 seconds. DON'T burn garlic.			

Add and stir-fry one minute...			*mussels*
Add...	$1/2$	cup	*dry white wine*
Stirfry 30 seconds. Add...	2	cups	*chicken stock*
Cover and steam for 2 minutes.			

In small bowl, mix together...

1/4	cup	*water*
3	tablespoons	*cornstarch*

Stir into mussels to thicken
broth slightly.

Garnish with sliced *green onions* and serve. Remember, you can do this in two batches if your pan is not large enough to cook all mussels at once; just cut all the ingredients in half to do two batches.

*Available in specialty sections of grocers; or see Spice Merchant (Participating Restaurants Index, page v).

MOO-PHI DRAGON
Serves 4

For this recipe, you will need...

6	ounces	**bay scallops,** blanched
		fresh ginger, sliced

Blanching the scallops before adding them to the recipe cooks them slightly, thereby removing some moisture which would otherwise escape into and ruin the sauce. In sauce pot, bring 3 quarts water and 2 slices of fre*sh ginger* to a boil. Drop scallops into boiling water for about 30 seconds. Remove scallops and place in ice cold water immediately. Drain scallops well.

In wok or sauté pan, over medium
high heat, combine...

		blanched scallops
3	ounces	**soy bean oil,** heated
6	ounces	**chicken breast meat,** diced into small bite-size pieces
6	ounces	**shrimp,** peeled, deveined

Stir and cook until shrimp have
just turned white. Remove from
pan and keep warm.

Drain oil from wok, wipe clean,

place over heat again and add...

3	ounces	*soy bean oil*
4	ounces	*snow peas*
3	large	*shitake mushrooms* sliced in long strips
1	small can	*water chestnuts,* sliced

Cook vegetables slightly and add...

seafood and chicken

2	tablespoons	*garlic,* minced

Stir-fry for a few moments.
DON'T burn garlic. Add...

3	ounces	*dry white wine*

Cook slightly and add...

6	ounces	*chicken stock**

Bring to a boil and stir in...

2	tablespoons	*oyster sauce* (no MSG)

In small bowl, mix together...

$1/4$	cup	*water*
3	tablespoons	*cornstarch*

Stir into wok to thicken
broth slightly.

Serve immediately with rice.

Homemade is best (see index for recipe); or good quality chicken base with water or canned broth.

THAI FRIED RICE
Serves 4-6

Preparation for this side dish should begin the day before, as the rice must be cooked and then allowed to dry before the final cooking process takes place.

The **day before** serving this dish,
in saucepan, combine...

4$^1/_2$	cups	*water*
3	cups	*short grain white rice,* rinsed twice with cold water

Bring to a boil, cover and simmer over low heat 10-12 minutes. Spread cooked rice out on a sheet pan; allow to cool to room temperature and dry. Cover and refrigerate overnight.

In wok, add...	2 tablespoons	*soy bean oil,* heated
	6 ounces	*shrimp,* chopped
Cook just until shrimp are turning white.		

Add...	4 ounces	*cellophane noodles,* soaked
	4 ounces	*black fungus*,* soaked
Stir-fry briefly.		

Add...	1 tablespoon	*fresh ginger,* grated
	1 tablespoon	*dry red chili flakes*
Then add...		*cooked rice*
	$^1/_2$ cup	*cooked eggs,* chopped
	$^1/_4$ cup	*green onions,* sliced
Stir-fry until hot.		

Add...	1 tablespoon	*sesame oil*
	2 tablespoons	*Thai fish sauce*
	1 tablespoon	*Vietnamese chili paste*

Stir-fry one minute longer and stir in...	2 tablespoons	*fresh mint,* chopped

Serve immediately.

*Available in specialty sections of grocers; or see Spice Merchant, page v.

chas

The Mangy Moose first opened in 1967 in Teton Village of Jackson Hole. It has grown over the years to become a most popular restaurant and saloon. The dining room and saloon have a fascinating atmosphere, filled with antiques and unusual memorabilia. Introducing Jackson Hole to its first salad bar, the Moose is still a step ahead, and unique in the country, by offering small portions of almost all of its entrees for light eaters.

The saloon was the first in the area to introduce its own brand of lager beer, known as Moose Brew. A variety of entertainment, from comedy acts to performers such as Leo Kottke, Blues Traveler and George Thorogood, are regular events in the saloon.

In addition to fine food and entertainment, the Mangy Moose houses a number of interesting shops offering antiques, Jackson Hole souvenirs, a full package liquor store and much more.

MENU FOR FOUR

Buffalo Crustini with Chipotle Mayonnaise

recommended wine ~ dry, crisp, bordeaux style white
Beringer Alluvium Blanc

Margarita Grilled Rainbow Trout

recommended wine ~ chardonnary with light oak and hint of fruit
Ferrari-Carano Chardonnay

Rice Pilaf

Seasonal Vegetable

Chocolate Huckleberry Pate

recommended wine ~ rich, full-bodied port with hint of chocolate and coffee
Warre's Warrior Port

Chef Hampton Ervolina

Wine pairings by The Wine Loft

BUFFALO CRUSTINI with
CHIPOTLE GORGONZOLA

Serves 4

For this recipe, you will need...	1	pound	*buffalo steak**
			olive oil
			salt and pepper

Brush *buffalo tenderloin* with *olive oil,* season with *salt and pepper.* Cook on hot grill to rare or medium rare. Remove from heat, allow to cool. Slice into $1/4$" slices.

| Lightly grill, on both sides... | 16 | slices | *French baguette,* |
| *(croutons)* | | | $1/4$" slices |

In small bowl, combine...	10	ounces	*gorgonzola cheese,*
			crumbled
	3	tablespoons	*mayonnaise*
	1	teaspoon	*chipotle pepper,*
			finely minced

Top each crouton with 1 or 2 slices buffalo; top with gorgonzola mixture. Set crustinis on baking sheet, place in **preheated** 500° oven for 2-3 minutes, or until cheese mixture is slightly browned. Serve immediately.

*Available at Jackson Hole Buffalo Meat Co. (See Participating Restaurants Index, page v)

MARINATED GRILLED RAINBOW TROUT

Serves 4

Start this the day before...the trout should marinate at least 6-8 hours; overnight is even better.

In large dish, combine...	8	ounces	*Jose Cuervo*
			Margarita Mix
(marinade)			(ready made)
	3	ounces	*Gold Tequila*
	$1/4$	cup	*fresh cilantro,*
			roughly chopped
	$1/2$	teaspoon	*salt*
	$1/2$	teaspoon	*pepper*

Place into marinade... 4 **8-10 ounce** *Rainbow Trout filets*
all bones removed

Marinate 6-8 hours or
overnight for best results.

Remove trout from marinade; spray flesh side of trout with generous amount of pan spray. Place on **very hot** grill, flesh side down. Cook 4-6 minutes, or until trout can be turned with ease (if trout sticks, cook longer). Cook on other side 3-6 minutes longer, until done. Remove from heat, brush top with *melted butter.* Serve immediately.

CHOCOLATE HUCKLEBERRY PATÉ   Serves 4

It is important to use a high quality chocolate to make this dessert.

In stainless steel bowl, place... 1 **pound** *semi-sweet chocolate*
finely chopped

Make sure bowl is completely
dry before placing chocolate in
it. DO NOT get any water in
the chocolate.

Place bowl to rest over the top of a pot with about $1/2$" boiling water. Using a rubber spatula, stir chocolate continuously until melted. DO NOT heat over 100°F.

In saucepan, combine...	$1/2$	**cup**	*heavy cream*
	2	**tablespoons**	*dark rum*
	1	**pinch**	*salt*

Heat to scald.

Fold hot cream mixture into chocolate (do not whisk). Stir gently until smooth.

Fold in...	4	**ounces**	*butter,* room temperature,
	1/2	**cup**	*huckleberries**

Do not overmix.

While mixture is still warm, pour into a small loaf pan (4" deep x 6" long) which has been prepared as follows: spray pan with pan spray, then line with plastic wrap, smoothing out any wrinkles [this insures the plastic will stay smooth and adhere to pan while pouring in the chocolate].

Chill paté in refrigerator for 6 hours. To serve, remove plastic and slice into $1/4$" slices, using a hot, dry knife.

Available at Rocky Mountain Huckleberry Co. (See Participating Restaurants Index, page v)

chas

Michael Burke opened the Cowboy Steakhouse in the lower level of the Million Dollar Cowboy Bar in 1995. Classically trained in Europe 30 years ago, and having been the chef at another fine restaurant in Jackson Hole, Michael developed the creative talent with which he established the finest steakhouse in Jackson.

Specializing in steaks and game, fresh pasta and seafood, the Cowboy Steakhouse treats its guests to casual dining in a rustic, yet elegant atmosphere. Guests will enjoy strolling down the long 'museum' entry hall, with its historic photographs and memorabilia of the Million Dollar Cowboy Bar dating all the way back to the early 1930s. It is a fascinating chapter of Jackson Hole history.

Much of the Steakhouse menu is created from Michael's recipes. However, during the last two years, Randy Alfano has been Chef of the Cowboy Steakhouse. Randy's own recipes are shared with us here!

MENU FOR SIX

Shrimp Louisiana

recommended wine - creamy, oaky chardonnay with hint of vanilla
Gallo of Sonoma Chardonnay

Wild Baby Greens
with Orange-Ginger Vinaigrette

Supreme Chicken Alfano with Fondant Potatoes

recommended wine - silky chardonnay with blended fruit flavors
Chalk Hill Chardonnay

Whole Baby Carrots Vichy

Bittersweet Chocolate Bread Pudding
with White Chocolate Sauce

recommended wine - sweet dessert wine with huckleberry and blackberry
Elysium

Chef Randy Alfano

Wine pairings by The Wine Loft

SHRIMP LOUISIANA Serves 6

This is so good, you could start and finish your meal with three helpings of these shrimp! You will wow your friends with Michael's presentation.

Peel and devein...	12	large	*shrimp* (keep tails on)
Dredge in...			*flour,* seasoned with salt and pepper
In sauté pan, over medium high flame, heat...	4	tablespoons	*butter,* clarified
Add **shrimp** and sauté very quickly. Add...	1 ½	tablespoons	*shallots,* chopped fine
	1	tablespoon	*garlic,* minced
Cook 1 minute.			
Add...	1	ounce	*pistachios,* peeled, chopped
Cook 1 minute and add...	2	tablespoons	*whole grain mustard*
And flambe with...	¼	cup	*vodka*
Add...	1	cup	*heavy cream*
Reduce by one third.			
Adjust seasoning with...			*salt and pepper to taste*
To complete recipe, you will need...	½	cup	*carrots,* julienned
(for garnish)	6		*scallion roses*

To serve, arrange three shrimp in center of each plate, on their backs with tails in the air facing edge of plate. Ladle sauce over shrimp and garnish with scallion and carrots. Serve immediately.

WILD BABY GREENS
with ORANGE GINGER VINAIGRETTE

Serves 6

Rinse, drain well and chill...	8	cups	*assorted baby greens*
In large salad bowl, with greens, toss together...	1	cup	*golden raisins*
	1/2	cup	*walnuts,* chopped
	1	cup	*green and red apples,* sliced*
	1/2 to 1	cup	*Orange-Ginger Vinaigrette*

If preparing ahead, dip apple slices in a lemon water bath to prevent them from turning brown.

Orange Ginger Vinaigrette

In mixing bowl, blend together...	1/4	cup	*rice vinegar*
	1/4	cup	*balsamic vinegar*
	2		*oranges,* juice of
	1	tablespoon	*shallots,* minced
	1	tablespoon	*fresh ginger,* minced
	1	cup	*peanut oil*

SUPREME CHICKEN ALFANO

Serves 6

Season with salt and pepper...	6	6-8 ounce	*chicken breasts,* boneless
Dredge chicken in...			*flour*

In large sauté pan, over medium flame, heat...	$1/4$	cup	*clarified butter*
Add...			*chicken breasts*
Sauté for two minutes.			

Turn chicken and top with...	6	slices	*swiss cheese*
Add...	$1 1/2$	tablespoons	*garlic,* minced
	$1 1/2$	tablespoons	*shallots,* minced
	6	tablespoons	*pinenuts,* toasted
	6	tablespoons	*ripe olives,* chopped
	6	tablespoons	*tomato concasse**
	2	tablespoons	*fresh basil,* chopped
	$1/4$	cup	*heavy cream*
			salt and pepper to taste
Reduce sauce by half.			

Serve immediately with sauce draped over chicken.

Finely diced fresh tomatoes (seeded).

FONDANT POTATOES Serves 6

Fondant potatoes are traditionally turned (trimmed with a knife) into barrel shapes of equal size and dimension. Over the years Michael has used baby white potatoes instead, achieving the same result.

In large baking dish, place...	18-24	turned	*baby white potatoes*
Add...	1	pint	*chicken stock*
	1	cup	*dry white wine*

Cover baking dish and place in **preheated** 350° oven for approximately 45 minutes.

WHOLE BABY CARROTS VICHY Serves 6

In large saucepan, combine...	1 1/2	pounds	*baby carrots,* tops on
	1	litre	*Vichy Water**
	1/2	pound	*unsalted butter*

Bring to a boil. Cover and simmer until al dente, about 15 minutes.

*Vichy Water is obtainable in gourmand shops. If no Vichy is avilable, combine 1/2 cup sugar with 1 litre quality bottled water.

BITTERSWEET CHOCOLATE BREAD PUDDING
with WHITE CHOCOLATE SAUCE Serves 6-8

This is also delicious as a white chocolate bread pudding with bittersweet chocolate sauce. Simply substitute white chocolate for the bittersweet chocolate in the bread pudding recipe; and substitute bittersweet chocolate for the white chocolate in the sauce recipe.

In large mixing bowl, place	7	cups	*brioche,* cut into cubes

In saucepan, combine...	1	cup	*heavy cream*
	3/4	cup	*sugar*
	1	pinch	*salt*
Bring to a scald. Remove from heat. Add..	12	ounces	*bittersweet chocolate* chopped
Allow to sit a couple of minutes, then whisk until smooth.			

In mixing bowl, combine...	2	large	*eggs*
	2		*egg yolks*
Whisk together until it is shiny and ribbon-like. Add...	2	cups	*whole milk*
	1	tablespoon	*vanilla extract*
Mix in...			*chocolate mixture*

Pour chocolate custard over broken up brioche. Let stand two hours at room temperature. Pour into buttered baking dish. Place baking dish in water bath and bake in **preheated** 325° oven for one hour. Allow to cool half an hour before serving. It will be very hot!

White Chocolate Sauce

| In mixing bowl which will sit over simmering water in saucepan, melt... | 8 | ounces | *white chocolate,* chopped |
| In saucepan, bring to boil... | 2 | cups | *heavy cream* |

Pour over melted white chocolate; cover really tight with plastic wrap and allow to stand 5 minutes. Remove plastic and whisk together until really smooth. Set bowl in ice water bath for 15 minutes to cool completely.

| When cold, add... | 1/2 | teaspoon | *pure vanilla extract* |

chas

Dining in the Mural Dining Room at the Jackson Lake Lodge is something most people will never forget. With its Rocky Mountain cuisine and breathtaking, panoramic view of Jackson Lake, Mount Moran and the entire Grand Teton range, a memorable evening awaits each guest. It is no wonder that the Mural Dining Room is also a favorite of Jackson Hole locals.

A full service resort right in the middle of Grand Teton National Park, Jackson Lake Lodge keeps its guests as busy as they wish. It's hard to beat just sitting in the Lodge's massive, spectacular lobby, looking out the two-story wall of windows, watching eagles soar and moose munch on the willows at the edge of Jackson Lake. For anyone ready for action, fishing, horseback riding, scenic and white water river trips, cruises on Jackson Lake, canoeing, and hiking are just some of the activities guests can choose from. Extraordinary meeting and conference facilities are also available.

The man responsible for so deliciously satisfying your hunger while at the Lodge, is Executive Chef Joseph Santangini. As an apprentice in the Rockresorts culinary program in 1984, Chef Joseph cooked at Jackson Lake Lodge under the tutelage of Robert Walton. Fifteen years later, in 1999, Chef Joseph returned to Jackson Lake Lodge as Executive Chef for the Grand Teton Lodge Company!

MENU FOR SIX

Baby Spring Greens
with Lemon Tarragon Vinaigrette

Mushroom Strudel

recommended wine ~ light, dry sauvignon or fume blanc with lots of citrus
Chateau St. Jean Fume Blanc

Marinated Lamb Chops with English Mint Sauce

recommended wine ~ very dry, bold red bordeaux or cabernet with big plum flavor
Francis Coppola Claret

White Chocolate Mousse Cake

recommended wine ~ light, very smooth port with berry flavor
Dows 20yr Tawny Port

Chef Joseph Santangini

Wine pairings by The Wine Loft

BABY SPRING GREENS
with LEMON TARRAGON VINAIGRETTE   Serves 6

For this recipe, you will need...	2	large bunches	*spring greens of choice*
	$^1/_2$	cup	*carrot,* curled or grated
			cherry tomatoes
			pine nuts, toasted (optional)

Rinse greens and drain well. Toss greens with *carrot* and Lemon Tarragon Vinaigrette. Portion out to salad plates. Garnish with *cherry tomatoes* and sprinkle with *toasted pine nuts.*

Lemon Tarragon Vinaigrette

In mixing bowl, place...	4	large	*egg yolks*
Whisk egg yolks			
until they froth. Add...	1	teaspoon	*fresh lemon juice*
	1	teaspoon	*rice wine vinegar*

| While whisking, slowly add... | 1 $^1/_2$ | cups | *olive oil* |
| | 1 $^1/_2$ | cups | *vegetable oil* |

Add...	3	tablespoons	*fresh lemon juice*
	3	tablespoons	*rice wine vinegar*
	3 T + 1	teaspoon	*white wine* (chablis)
	$^1/_2$	teaspoon	*garlic,* minced
	$^3/_4$	teaspoon	*shallots,* minced
	1$^1/_2$	teaspoons	*tarragon*
	1$^1/_2$	teaspoons	*salt*
	$^3/_4$	teaspoon	*white pepper*

Chill until ready for use.

MUSHROOM STRUDEL

Serves 6

For this recipe, you will need...	6	sheets	*phyllo dough*
	1/2	cup	*butter,* melted

In sauté pan, over medium
    heat, combine...

	1	cup	*white wine*
	1	pound	*shitake mushrooms,* sliced
	1	pound	*wild mushrooms,* sliced
	1	teaspoon	*garlic,* minced

Sauté for about 2 minutes.
Drain and cool.

In mixing bowl, combine...	1/2	cup	*Béchamel Sauce*
	2	large	*egg yolks*

Add to mushrooms (only
enough to coat).

Place one sheet phyllo dough on cool board. Brush lightly, but evenly, with *melted butter*. Place another sheet phyllo dough on top and brush with butter. Repeat process again until you have three layers buttered phyllo dough. Place cooled mushroom mixture on dough in a thick line across length. Roll up. Brush with melted butter. Place strudel, seam side down, on a non-stick pan. Bake in **preheated** 350° oven until golden brown, about 15 minutes. Take out of oven and let set for 5 minutes. Using a **sharp** knife, slice strudel into servings. Serve hot.

Bechamel Sauce

In saucepan, combine...	3	tablespoons	*butter,* melted
	6	tablespoons	*flour*

Stir briskly until smoothly
blended, without allowing
it to brown or change color.

Gradually add, while			
whisking...	2	cups	*milk,* heated to boiling
Whisk well to prevent any			
lumps forming. Then add...	1	pinch	*salt*
	1	pinch	*white pepper*
	1	pinch	*nutmeg* (optional)

Over medium heat, continue cooking, while stirring, until sauce has thickened. Allow to cool. Cover any unused portion for use at another time.

MARINATED LAMP CHOPS Serves 6

Lamb chops should be approximately 4 ounces each, trimmed of all fat.

For this recipe, you will need...	12		*lamb chops*
	3		*pears,* peeled, halved
			fresh mint leaves

In mixing bowl, combine...	1/2	cup	*olive oil*
	2	tablespoons	*fresh basil,* chopped
(marinade)	2	tablespoons	*fresh rosemary,* leaves only, chopped
	2	tablespoons	*fresh thyme,* leaves only, chopped
	2	tablespoons	*white peppercorns,* crushed

Marinate lamb chops for 4 hours. Broil or grill to desired doneness. To serve, place grilled chops on dinner plate with pear half filled with English Mint Sauce and garnished with fresh *mint leaf.*

English Mint Sauce

Rinse well to clean and discard stems of...	1¼	pounds	*fresh mint*
Finely chop mint.			

In small bowl, combine...	1	cup	*white vinegar*
	4	tablespoons	*apple cider*
This forms an *apple cider vinegar*. Set aside until ready to use.			

In saucepan, over medium heat, combine...	2	tablespoons	*water*
	1¼	cups	*sugar*
Melt sugar, stirring occasionally. Add...			*apple cider vinegar* *chopped mint*

Mix well. Allow to set for 30 minutes at room temperature. Refrigerate to chill.

To finish sauce, combine chilled mint mixture with equal amounts of *apple cider vinegar* and *melted sugar*.

WHITE CHOCOLATE MOUSSE CAKE

Serves 10

In mixing bowl, combine...	10 $\frac{1}{2}$	ounces	*cake flour*
	10	ounces	*sugar*
	$\frac{3}{4}$	teaspoon	*baking soda*
	$\frac{3}{4}$	teaspoon	*salt*
Slowly, whisk in...	1 $\frac{1}{2}$	large	*eggs*

Stir in...	1	cup	*vegetable oil*
	$\frac{1}{2}$	cup	*buttermilk*
	$\frac{3}{4}$	teaspoon	*white vinegar*
	3	drops	*yellow food color*

Pour into greased and floured cake pans. Bake in **preheated** 375° oven for approximately 25 minutes, until toothpick inserted in center comes out clean. Allow cakes to cool completely. Assemble cake with White Chocolate Filling and White Chocolate Topping.

White Chocolate Filling

In top of double boiler, melt...	8	ounces	*white chocolate,* broken into pieces
Fold in...	12	ounces	*whipped topping*

White Chocolate Topping

In top of double boiler, melt...	20	ounces	*white chocolate,* broken into pieces
In saucepan, bring to a boil...	1	cup	*heavy cream*

Add hot cream to melted white chocolate. Blend well.

chas

Nani's Genuine Pasta House serves only truly authentic, regional Italian food and pastries, made in their kitchen in the 'Old Country' way, from natural and fresh ingredients. Each month Nani's chef, Melissa Phillips, features a menu from a different region. It is the desire of Nani's owner, Carol Mortillaro Parker, to raise the consciousness of American diners as to the authentic taste of Italian food. Carol's philosophy includes the belief that every person is a VIP. To dine in Nani's is to experience a little piece of Italy!

At Nani's you will be treated to a most pleasurable and educational dining experience. When I asked asked Carol what information she would like me to include when writing about her restaurant, she directed me to her web page for ideas. Nani's web page is so filled with interesting history, stories, and information about regional Italian cuisine, that I recommend everyone to 'travel' to www.nanis.com.

While at Nani's webpage, I found myself fondly reminiscing about the week I spent 'eating my way' through Italy some twenty years ago. If you've always wanted to go to Italy, or if you've been fortunate enough to travel to Italy and experience its magnificent cuisine, be sure to visit Nani's. Close your eyes and you will feel as though you are in Italy!

As guests repeatedly ask for Nani's sausage (salsicce) recipes, Carol and Melissa decided to share three of them here, along with other selected favorite recipes.

Salsicce da Umbria

Salsicce da Basilicata

Salsicce da Trentino Alto Adige

recommended wine - lightly spiced chianti with dark fruit
Ecco Domani Sangiovese

Limoncello

Cozze con Vino

recommended wine - light, dry pinot gris with peach and pear
Sartori Pinot Grigio

Fettuccine al Pollo e Salvia

recommended wine - very fruitful, smooth Italian syrah with light berry
Allegrini Palazzo Della Torre

Penne ai Quattro Formaggi

recommended wine - peppery chianti with medium body and light dryness
Banfi Risierva Chianti Classico

Chef Melissa Phillips
Wine Pairings by The Wine Loft

"If everyone knew how easy it is to make sausage, the butcher would surely be saddened. Here are a few recipes to get started with, based on the regional recipes we have developed at Nani's. Feel free once you have made the sausage to try out different spices and amounts of those spices. Don't forget to take notes though, or you might create something wonderful that you cannot duplicate."

Basic Sausage Making

1.   **Always use freshly ground spices.**** "Most spices in our homes are years old. Throw them out, buy new, and grind fresh in your (clean) coffee grinder for each recipe."
2.   Never use lean ground meat in sausage making. There should always be 20% fat in the meat. ["Trust me, I learned the hard way."]
3.   In these recipes I do not go into casing. You will need special equipment to put your sausages into casings.
4.   Sausage must have salt in it, so do not try to cut back on the salt, as the sausage will not turn out properly.

SALSICCE da UMBRIA

In container, combine...	1	pound	*black seedless grapes*
			(organic)
	1/4	cup	*cognac or Grappa*

Soak grapes overnight.
Drain well. Dice grapes.

Mix together...			*grapes*
	5	pounds	*ground pork*
	2	tablespoons	*fennel seed***
	1/4	cup	*salt*
	1/4	cup	*black pepper***
	1	tablespoon	*allspice***
	1/4	cup	*red wine vinegar*
	1	cup	*red wine*
	1	tablespoon	*fresh garlic,* chopped

Mix well. Fry a little, to taste for seasoning, before continuing. Adjust seasoning. Use in sauces or form into patties.

SALSICCE da BASILICATA

**See notes on sausage making on previous page. Especially note that all spices should be freshly ground.*

In food processor, mix together
until well combined...

¹/₂	cup	*pancetta,* chopped
¹/₄"	piece	*fresh ginger,* peeled, crushed
1	tablespoon	*fresh garlic,* minced

Mix together...

		pancetta mixture
5	pounds	*ground pork*
³/₄	cup	*dry red wine*
¹/₄	cup	*Grappa*
1	tablespoon	*kosher salt*
1	teaspoon	*white pepper***

Mix well. Fry a little, to taste for seasoning, before continuing. Adjust seasoning. Use in sauces or shape into medium patties.

SALSICCE da TRENTINO ALTO ADIGE

**See notes on sausage making on previous page. Especially note that all spices should be freshly ground.*

Mix together...

5	pounds	*ground pork*
¹/₄	cup	*fresh garlic,* chopped
¹/₄	cup	*dry white wine*
2	tablespoons	*black pepper***
1¹/₂	tablespoon	*kosher salt*
1	teaspoon	*caraway seeds*
¹/₄	teaspoon	*nutmeg***
¹/₄	teaspoon	*paprika*

LIMONCELLO *(a vodka-lemon drink)*

Wash and peel (leaving no white pith)...	15	thick-skinned	*lemons*
In glass container with tight fitting lid, combine...			*lemons*
	2	750 ml	*vodka* (high quality)
Leave *limoncello* in dark place for 40 days.			
On 40th day, in saucepan combine...	5	cups	*water*
	4	cups	*sugar*
Bring to boil and cook until thickened, about 5 minutes.			

Let syrup mixture cool completely. Mix in *limoncello*. Leave in dark place for another 40 days. Strain. Keep in freezer. Enjoy!

COZZE con VINO *(Mussels with Wine)*   Serves 4

Use only the freshest Prince Edward Island Mussels. Be sure to have fresh, crusty bread to sop up the juices!

In food processor, or with mortar and pestle, grind together...	1/4	cup	*fresh garlic,* minced
	2	tablespoons	*red pepper flake*
	3	ounces	*anchovy* (canned)
Add...	1	cup	*fresh oregano,* leaves only, no stems
	1	bunch	*flat leaf parsley*
Grind again until a paste forms.			

| Whisk in... | 1/4 | cup | *extra virgin olive oil* |

[Use approximately 1 teaspoon of this paste per pound of mussels when cooking]]

In large pot, place...	2	teaspoons	*paste*
On top of paste, add...	2	pounds	*Prince Edward Island Mussels*
Pour in...	2	cups	*dry white wine* (fume or sauvignon blanc)

Cover, steam until all mussels open. Stir and give each serving of mussels plenty of the juices. Serve with fresh, crusty bread.

FETTUCCINE al POLLO e SALVIA   Serves 4-6

A great way to use your leftover cooked chicken. Or cook your favorite cut in 350° oven with a little salt and pepper until just barely cooked through (don't worry if you see pink spots, as you will cook it a little more later.

| For this recipe you will need... | 1 | pound | *fettuccine,* cooked al dente in plenty of salted water |
| Keep warm or reheat in hot water bath (drain well). | | | |

In large sauté pan, heat...	1/2	cup	*extra virgin olive oil*
Add...	20	whole	*fresh sage leaves* (do not use dried)
	1	zest of	*lemon*
It should sizzle quickly.			

Stir in...	1	pound	*cooked chicken meat*
Add...	1	tablespoon	*fresh garlic,* chopped or thinly sliced
Stir, and do not let garlic burn.			

Sprinkle over mixture...	1	cup	*bread crumbs*

Stir and let bread crumbs brown a little. Add all at once...	1$^{1}/_{2}$	cups	*chicken stock** *salt and pepper to taste*

Toss with hot fettuccine pasta.

*Homemade is best (see index for recipe; or good quality, low-salt canned.

PENNE ai QUATTRO FORMAGGI

Serves four for dinner, or six as first course. **All cheeses used in this recipe must be freshly grated just prior to preparation.**

In saucepan, heat...	10	ounces	*heavy cream*
	4	ounces	*Parmigiana-Reggiano cheese*
	4	ounces	*Pecorino-Romano cheese [OR] Locatelli-Romano*
	4	ounces	*Italian Fontina cheese [OR] Asiago cheese*
	8	ounces	*Italian Gorgonzola cheese [OR] Gorgonzola Dolce*
Stir occasionally until melted.			

Cook, according to instructions...	1	pound	*Italian Penne Rigate pasta*
Drain well.			

Toss pasta and cheese sauce together. Serve with freshly ground black pepper.

In the summer of 1986 Off Broadway opened its doors featuring a classy yet casual atmosphere, an open kitchen, two intimate dining rooms and a private banquet room with balcony. Located in the heart of downtown Jackson, just off the town square, Off Broadway boasts a large deck for summer dining, always a delight with its array of flowers and quiet surroundings.

The success of Off Broadway is a result of the consistent high quality of the foods presented, the creative and varied menus, and the friendly and professional staff. Off Broadway chefs focus on lighter fare, creating imaginative foods for healthy appetites.

Changing with the seasons, their menu offers a variety of traditional and inventive recipes. On any given night, entrees may be complemented by sauces such as Italian pesto, French beurre blanc, Thai peanut sauce, Caribbean lime sauce, or Mexican roasted chili salsa. Known primarily for grilled seafood and a variety of pastas, Off Broadway also serves a selection of choice meats, poultry and wild game.

Open for dinner year around, Off Broadway also offers private catering. Complementing its food is a wide selection of fine wines, cocktails, gourmet coffees and espresso. In keeping with their imaginative flair with seafood specialties, Chef Belliveau has given us a selection of three very different seafood entrees, plus a wonderful elk dish.

FEATURED RECIPES

Grilled Caribbean Prawns

recommended wine ~ very silky, white meritage with honeydew melon
Caymus Conundrum

Seared Ahi
with Wasabi Vinaigrette

recommended wine ~ lightly spiced gerwurztraminer with medium fruit, vanilla and oak
Gundlach-Bundschu Gerwurztraminer

Herb Encrusted Salmon
with Sundried Tomato Vinaigrette

recommended wine ~ silky chardonnay with blended fruit flavors
Chalk Hill Chardonnay

Braised Elk Osso Bucco

recommended wine ~ big, full-bodied Italian Tuscan
Castello Banfi Brunello di Montalcino

Chef Alan Belliveau

Wine pairings by The Wine Loft

GRILLED CARIBBEAN PRAWNS

This is a super recipe which can be used to prepare shrimp as a party hors d'oeurve, a first course, or grilled on skewers as a main entree.

For this recipe you will need...	2	pounds	*large prawns,* peeled and deveined

In mixing bowl, blend together...	$^1/_4$	cup	*dark rum*
	$^1/_4$	cup	*fresh lime juice*
(marinade)	$^1/_4$	cup	*soy sauce*
	$^1/_4$	cup	*extra virgin olive oil*
	2	tablespoons	*fresh ginger,* minced
	$^1/_4$	cup	*brown sugar*
	1	teaspoon	*nutmeg*
	$^1/_2$	teaspoon	*allspice*
	$^1/_2$	teaspoon	*cinnamon*

Marinate prawns for two hours. Remove prawns from *marinade* and grill until done. When the seam along the back has just changed from opaque to white, they are perfect. Serve warm.

[Reserve marinade and heat to serve as dipping sauce with prawns.]

SEARED AHI with WASABI VINAIGRETTE   *Serves 4-6 as appetizer*

For sashimi lovers, here is a fabulous first course that is so quick and easy!

For this recipe you will need...	1	pound	*ahi tuna* (fresh sashimi grade)
	8	ounces	*pickled Asian cabbage*
	2	ounces	*pickled ginger*

Blend together in a food processor...	1/4	cup	*tahini*
	1/4	cup	*rice wine vinegar*
(vinaigrette)	1/4	cup	*wasabi*
	1/2	tablespoon	*dijon mustard*
	1/2	tablespoon	*white sugar*
	1	tablespoon	*soy sauce*

Sear tuna in a hot skillet for one minute on each side. Slice. To serve, portion out *pickled cabbage* onto serving plates, top with slices of ahi, and drizzle vinaigrette over the top. Garnish with *pickled ginger*.

HERB ENCRUSTED SALMON
with SUNDRIED TOMATO VINAIGRETTE

Serves 4

One of Chef Belliveau's newly created specialties! Be sure to make the Sundried Tomato Vinaigrette **two or three days ahead of time.**

For this recipe, you will need...	2	pounds	*salmon filets*
	2	cups	*bread crumbs*

In small mixing bowl, combine...	2	tablespoons	*dijon mustard*
	1	tablespoon	*fresh tarragon*
	1	tablespoon	*fresh thyme*
	1	tablespoon	*fresh basil*

Coat salmon filets with mustard-herb mixture, then cover with bread crumbs. In a saute pan, on high heat, sear salmon on both sides until golden brown. Place salmon in **pre-heated** 350° oven for 15-20 minutes to finish. Serve salmon draped with Sundried Tomato Vinaigrette (be sure to stir the vinaigrette well just before serving).

Sundried Tomato Vinaigrette

Two or three days ahead of time,
    mix together...

	1	cup	*extra virgin olive oil*
	1/3	cup	*balsamic vinegar*
(vinaigrette)	2	tablespoons	*water*
	1	whole	*shallot,* chopped
	1/2	cup	*sundried tomatoes,** julienned

Making the vinaigrette well ahead of time allows the sundried tomatoes to plump up.

BRAISED ELK OSSO BUCCO   Serves 6-8

Pop this in the oven and leave for three hours. Go for a short hike on a fall or winter's day, or run a few errands. Then come home to relax and enjoy a good meal!

One to two days ahead...

In a large saucepan, combine...	1	cup	*red wine*
	1	whole	*onion,* chopped
Reduce by half.			

In food processor, grind...	1	large	*carrot*
	1	whole	*red pepper,* seeded
(sauce)	1	cup	*parsley,* lightly packed
	1	whole	*lemon,* seeded, peeled, pulp only

Add and blend...   *wine-onion reduction*
Place mixture in saucepan.

Add...	2	cups	*stewed tomatoes,* canned
	2	cups	*beef stock**
	1	tablespoon	*garlic,* minced
	1/4	cup	*white sugar*
Bring to a boil; then simmer for 2 hours.			

| To complete recipe, you will need... | 3 | pounds | *elk shank* |
| | | | *flour,* seasoned with salt and pepper |

Coat elk shank with seasoned *flour*. In hot skillet, sear elk on all sides. Place in deep baking dish, cover with *sauce*. Place cover on baking dish and bake in **preheated** 350° oven for 3 hours.

Homemade is best (see index for recipe). Or use a good quality beef base with water.

chas

Old Yellowstone Garage, "that western Italian ristorante!", had its beginnings in the small town of Dubois, Wyoming in 1994. Offering classic Piemontese Italian cuisine with a western influence, it became a favorite of Jackson locals and visitors alike.

It was so good, that Jackson residents would drive one and a half hours on mountain roads to have dinner there! Of course, it *is* a beautiful drive over Togwotee Pass. In fact, people loved the drive over. But after a long, leisurely meal (and probably some wine too), no one liked the drive home!

With such a large following of customers from Jackson, and after many suggestions and requests by customers to "....bring Old Yellowstone Garage to Jackson Hole", owners, David and Cinzia Gilbert did just that!

David and Cinzia have enjoyed huge success since opening the new doors of Old Yellowstone Garage in Jackson in 2000. With its beautiful interiors reminiscent of classic Piemonte, Italy, it has added a whole new look to the world of dining in Jackson Hole. Don't miss an opportunity to dine at the 'Garage!'

MENU FOR FOUR

Bagna Cauda

recommended wine - Italian white with light sweetness of honey and vanilla
Principessa Gavi

Brasata Al Barolo

recommended wine - rich, bold, full-bodied Italian red from Piedmont region
Borgogno Barolo

Polenta with Wild Mushrooms and Gorgonzola

recommended wine - big, rich, fruity Piedmont red with bold expansive body
Falletto Barbaresco

Chef David Gilbert

Wine pairings by The Wine Loft

BAGNA CAUDA
Serves 4

For this recipe, you will need...			*assorted vegetables for dipping....*
			carrots, red & yellow peppers, cooked potatoes, cauliflower
			crusty bread

In small bowl, combine...	5	cloves	*garlic,* crushed
	1/2	cup	*milk*
Soak garlic in milk to cover for one hour. Drain.			

In a non conductive pan (preferably earthenware), slowly heat...			*soaked garlic*
	1/2	cup	*extra virgin olive oil*
		a few drops	*walnut oil*
	1/4	cup	*anchovies,* rinsed
Be careful not to brown the garlic.			

After about 15 minutes, add...	1	tablespoon	*butter,* melted

Heat over very low temperature for one hour. Serve the sauce in a small chafing dish or fondue pot. Surround dish with an assortment of vegetables and crusty bread. Traditionally, fennel and cardoons are used, if they are available. Cardoon is a vegetable that grows like celery in bunches, with a suede like finish; a relative of the artichoke. Now there's a great vegetable to dip too! Feel free to experiment with any other vegetable that strikes your fancy.

BRASATO al BAROLO

Serves 4-6

In a non-reactive pan, combine...	2	tablespoons	*butter,* melted
	2-2¼	pounds	*rump roast*
	2	ounces	*pancetta* (Italian bacon)
	1	medium	*onion,* coarsely chopped
	1	clove	*garlic*
	1	medium	*carrot,* coarsely chopped
	1	stalk	*celery*
	1	sprig	*fresh rosemary*
	1	whole	*bay leaf*
	1	stick	*cinnamon*
			salt and pepper to taste

Brown meat on all sides.

| Add... | ¹/₂ | bottle | *barolo or barbera wine* |

| To complete recipe, you will need... | ¹/₂ | glass | *grappa* |

Cover and let it reduce slowly. (If necessary, add some warm water) Cook for about an hour and a half on low heat. Remove the meat; slice it into ¹/₂" pieces. Strain the liquid and place it and the sliced meat back in the pan. Add a half glass of *grappa* and cook for 15 minutes longer, on low to moderate heat, to reduce sauce. Serve immediately.

POLENTA with
WILD MUSHROOMS and GORGONZOLA

Serves 4

In large, non stick skillet, over medium flame, heat...	2 tablespoons	*extra virgin olive oil*
Add... Cook about two minutes, until shallots are translucent.	¹/₄ cup	*shallots,* minced
Add and sauté until brown and tender... Cook about 6 minutes, until liquid evaporates.	1 pound	*wild mushrooms* (or oyster, shitake, crimini, etc.)
Add... Simmer until port is reduced by one third, about 1 minute.	³/₄ cup	*ruby port*
Add... Reduce by one third; about 1 minute longer.	¹/₂ cup	*chicken stock* (or canned low-salt broth)
Remove skillet from heat and whisk in...	2 tablespoons	*unsalted butter,* room temperature, broken into pieces
Season with...		*salt and pepper* *to taste*

Can be prepared two hours ahead. Rewarm, over medium heat, before serving. Serve over
Polenta.

Polenta

For his polenta dishes, David prefers to use Taragna (buckwheat) polenta.

In large saucepan, combine...	4	cups	*water*
	1	cup	*polenta*
	1	teaspoon	*salt*

Whisk to blend and bring
mixture to a boil, whisking
constantly.

Add...	3	tablespoons	*unsalted butter,*
			room temperature,
			broken into pieces

Reduce heat to medium-low. Cook
until polenta is soft andthick,
whisking frequently, about 15 minutes.

Add...	1	cup	*gorgonzola cheese,*
			crumbled

Whisk until melted.

Spoon polenta into warm serving bowls. Spoon mushrooms over polenta and serve.

chas

One of my very favorite restaurants in Jackson, The Range has really come of age in the last ten years. Originally a small, intimate restaurant in Teton Village, The Range has relocated to 'downtown' Jackson and boasts a much larger, exquisitely beautiful dining room. Its theatre style kitchen still offers diners the opportunity to watch Chef Arthur Leech and his staff prepare their dinner.

Featured in numerous magazines, such as Town and Country, Bon Appetit, Gourmet, and Wine Spactator, Arthur developed his creative culinary talents as he worked under the tutelage of fine chefs early in his career. The menus featured at The Range are his innovative interpretation of American regional cuisine.

The menu and recipes Arthur shares with us here would make any dinner party a smashing success. Enjoy!

MENU FOR FOUR

Smoked Salmon Wrapped Ahi Tuna with Mango Curry Coconut Milk

recommended wine ~ 1996 Trimbach 'Cuvee Frederic Emile' Riesling

Savoy, Green Apple, Toasted Pistachios, Dry Aged Sonoma Jack Cheese, with Chardonnay Vinaigrette

recommended wine ~ 1997 Chateau Montelena Chardonnay

Rocky Mountain Elk Sirloin with Juniper-Rosemary Sauce

recommended wine ~ Domaine Des Perdrix Nuits Saint Georges Aux Perdrix

Goat Cheese Risotto

Lace Cookie Cups with Chocolate Sorbet

Chef Arthur Leech

Wine pairings by Arthur

SMOKED SALMON WRAPPED AHI TUNA
with MANGO CURRY COCONUT MILK   Serves 4

Arthur suggests a1996 Trimbach "Cuvee Frederic Emile" Riesling would be very nice with this ahi.

For this recipe you will need...	4	3-4 ounce	*ahi filets*
	6-8	ounces	*smoked salmon,*
			thinly sliced

Sear ahi filets in vegetable oil in an extremely hot skillet to desired doneness (rare is best!). Wrap each filet with thin slices of smoked salmon; then slice each diagonally through the center. Display on plate and drape with Mango Curry Coconut Milk.

Mango Curry Coconut Milk

In food processor or bowl,
blend well together...

10	ounces	*mango juice*
1/2	cup	*coconut milk*
2	tablespoons	*rice vinegar*
		(seasoned)
3	tablespoons	*apple juice*
2	tablespoons	*orange juice*
1	teaspoon	*curry paste*
	pinch	*salt*

SAVOY, GREEN APPLE, TOASTED PISTACHIOS and DRY AGED SONOMA JACK CHEESE with CHARDONNAY VINAIGRETTE

Serves 4

This is a terrific combination of textures and flavors...the dry aged jack cheese and green apple are wonderfully complemented by the character of a light, slightly acidic chardonnay which creates the vinaigrette. A 1997 Chateau Montelena Chardonnay would do nicely while you enjoy your salad.

Pull apart, rinse and drain well... Shred and julienne slice.	1/2	head	*Savoy cabbage*
Toast in skillet over medium high heat, shaking pan often until lightly browned...	1/	cup	*pistachios*
To complete recipe, you will need...	1	whole	*Granny Smith apple,* thinly sliced*
	1/2	cup	*Sonoma Jack Cheese,* julienned

Combine all ingredients in large salad bowl, dress with Chardonnary Vinaigrette and toss. Arrange on plates and serve.

If preparing ahead, dip apple slices in a lemon water bath to prevent them from turning brown.

Chardonnay Vinaigrette

Whisk together...	1 1/2	cups	*olive oil*
	1/2	cup	*rice vinegar*
	1/2	cup	*chardonnay*
	6	tablespoons	*apple juice*
			salt and pepper to taste
Blend for 2 minutes.			

ROCKY MOUNTAIN ELK SIRLOIN
with JUNIPER-ROSEMARY SAUCE

Serves 4

Arthur uses Rocky Mountain elk because of its fresher flavor. However it is not readily available except through select game purveyors. New Zealand elk or any other venison would be a fine substitute in this recipe. Because elk and venison are very lean, it can easily become dry when cooking, especially grilling. For that reason, Arthur pan sears the elk sirloins.

To complement this entree, Arthur would recommend a young burgandy, such as Domaine Des Perdrix Nuits Saint Georges Aux Perdrix.

In hot skillet, heat...	2	tablespoons	*olive oil*
Add and sear on both sides...	4	6-8 ounce	*elk sirloins,* $^3/_4$ " thick
Remove from pan and place in a pre**heated** 375° oven to finish cooking while preparing sauce.			
In same skillet, over medium high heat, add...	1	tablespoon	*shallots,* minced
	2	teaspoons	*garlic,* minced
Deglaze pan with...	$^1/_2$	cup	*brandy*
Reduce by one half and add...	$^1/_2$	cup	*beef demi-glace**
Reduce slightly to thicken			
Stir or swirl in until melded into sauce...	2	tablespoons	*compound butter,* cold, broken into pieces

[*Compound butter* is Arthur's blend of $^1/_2$ cup butter and 2 tablespoons each of finely chopped juniper berries and finely chopped fresh rosemary. This can be made well in advance and refrigerated.] Spoon sauce onto plate, place elk sirloin on top, along with portion of Goat Cheese Rissotto. Serve.

*Available in fine culinary stores/catalogs; or see index for recipe or quick substitutions.

GOAT CHEESE RISOTTO   Serves 4

In large saucepan, combine...	2	tablespoons	*butter*
	2	tablespoons	*olive oil*
	1	cup	*onion,* finely chopped
	1	clove	*garlic,* minced
Cook over moderate heat, stirring occasionally until onion is translucent.			

Add and stir until grains are coated with oil and rice is heated through...	1	cup	*Arborio rice*
Add and stir constantly until liquid is absorbed...	$^1/_2$	cup	*dry white wine*

To complete recipe, you will need...	$2^1/_2$	cups	*chicken broth,* kept hot over lowest simmer
	$^1/_4$	cup	*goat cheese*

When wine has been absorbed, add $^1/_2$ cup hot *chicken broth*, stirring often until liquid is absorbed. Continue adding broth $^1/_2$ cup at a time, stirring often and letting each portion be absorbed before adding the next, until rice is tender but still al dente (it should take about 17 minutes for the rice to become al dente). Just before serving, stir in *goat cheese.*

LACE COOKIE CUPS
with CHOCOLATE SORBET
Serves 4-6

Mary Koontz, baker for The Range, creates this terrific dessert. The chocolate sorbet is also delicious served with fruit, such as raspberries or blueberries!

In a heavy sauce pan, over medium
  high heat, bring to a boil...

3	tablespoons	*corn syrup*
4	tablespoons	*butter*
6	tablespoons	*brown sugar,* packed

Stir in...   7 tablespoons *flour*

Stir constantly until dough is
smooth. Cool to room temperature.

Scoop out cookie dough and flatten into 4" to 5" rounds on baking sheet. Bake in **preheated** 350° oven until golden, about 8-10 minutes.

Have inverted glasses ready. When cookies are done, take out of oven. Cool about 45 seconds; place cookies on bottom of glasses until cooled. Carefully remove from glasses. Serve with small scoops of Chocolate Sorbet.

Chocolate Sorbet   [makes about 1 quart]

In top of double boiler, melt...   7 ounces   *semi-sweet chocolate*
broken into pieces

When melted, stir in...   1 1/2 tablespoons   *vegetable oil*

In saucepan, bring to a boil...	2^1/$_4$ cups	*water*
	1/4 cup + 2 teaspoons	*sugar*

Cook 3 minutes.
Add and mix well...   *chocolate mixture*

Whisk in...

1/2	cup	*light corn syrup*
1/2	teaspoon	*vanilla*
	dash	*salt*

Blend well. Chill in refrigerator until cooled. Pour into ice cream maker. Follow manufacturer's instructions for freezing. When frozen, scoop into **Lace Cookie Cups**.

MENU FOR FOUR

Artichoke Heart Pate with Garlic Lemon Mayonnaise

recommended wine - 1998 Chalk Hill Sauvignon Blanc

Marinated Shitake Mushrooms

recommended wine - 1997 Henry Estate Pinot Noir

Shrimp and Scallop 'Stew'

recommended wine - Ferrari-Carano Siena

Warm Chocolate Bread Pudding with Bourbon Sauce

recommended wine - Graham's Vintage Port 1980

Chef Arthur Leech

Wine pairings by Arthur

ARTICHOKE HEART PATÉ
with GARLIC LEMON MAYONNAISE   Serves 4

Make this a day ahead, as it needs to be refrigerated overnight before serving. A perfect wine to enjoy with this pate would be a 1998 Chalk Hill Sauvignon Blanc.

In large shallow dish, combine. . .	2	cups	*dry bread,* chopped
	1	cup	*heavy cream*
Allow to stand until cream is completely absorbed, forming a paste ...'panache'.			

In food processor, combine			
and puree until smooth. . .	3	12 oz cans	*artichoke hearts,* drained
	$^1/_4$	cup	*dry white wine*
	1	tablespoon	*Dijon mustard* (grainy)
	1		*shallot,* finely chopped
			black pepper to taste,

With processor running, add. . .	2	large	*eggs,* one at a time

Puree until eggs are
completely incorporated.

Firmly pack paté mixture into a greased, springform paté pan. Place pan on a cookie sheet, wrap sides with damp towels and cover with foil. Bake in a **preheated** 325° oven for approximately two hours, until internal temperature reaches 180°. Remove from oven, keep covered with foil, but remove towels and allow to cool to room temperature before placing in refrigerator overnight. Serve with Garlic Lemon Mayonnaise and slices of fresh, crusty French bread.

Garlic Lemon Mayonnaise

In food processor, puree together. . .	1	large	*egg*
	1		*lemon,* juice of
	2	teaspoons	*fresh garlic,* crushed
			black pepper to taste, freshly ground

With processor running, add. . .	2	**cups**	*canola oil*

Before adding the final 1/4 cup of oil, test for consistency. Mayonnaise should be thick and able to hold soft peaks. Chill in refrigerator.

If you do not have a food processor, or you wish to prepare the mayonnaise in the classic tradition...

In a stainless steel bowl, combine the egg, lemon juice, garlic and pepper. 'Anchor' the bowl with a wet towel placed underneath. Slowly add the oil in a steady stream while beating continuously with a whisk. Adding the oil *very* slowly at first will initiate the emulsion. Continue adding the oil in a steady stream until the mayonnaise becomes thick and will hold soft peaks.

MARINATED SHITAKE MUSHROOMS
Serves 4

Arthur suggests a 1997 Henry Estate Pinot Noir to accompany this course.

For this recipe, you will need. . .	1	**head**	*romaine lettuce,* sliced into thin ribbons
	1	**large**	*tomato* (for garnish)

Steam for two minutes. . .	10	**large**	*shitake mushrooms,* thinly sliced

Immediately, while hot, place mushrooms into **vinaigrette marinade**.

Marinate mushrooms for at least three hours. To serve, arrange mushrooms on beds of *romaine ribbons*. Spoon additional vinaigrette over each portion and, if you wish, garnish with wedges or slices of *tomato*.

Vinaigrette Marinade

In bowl, combine. . .	1	**cup**	*olive oil*
	1/4	**cup**	*balsamic vinegar*
	2	**tablespoons**	*water*

Finely chop and add...	1	tablespoon	*fresh chives*
	1	tablespoon	*fresh thyme*
	1	tablespoon	*fresh basil*
			black pepper to taste, freshly ground

Mix the marinade well and stir occcasionally to keep it from separating until adding the mushrooms.

Variation

Marinate whole shitake mushrooms in vinaigrette, drain, place on skewers and grill over medium flame for 4-6 minutes. Serve warm.

SHRIMP and SCALLOP 'STEW'   Serves 4

This is a delicious dish for anyone watching their fat intake. There is no butter or cream in this recipe. For those who enjoy wine, a glass of Ferrari-Carano Siena will go nicely with the Stew.

For this recipe, you will need...	1	large	*leek* (white only)
	1	large	*tomato,* smoked*
	2	tablespoons	*pine nuts,* toasted**

Rub leek with oil, roast in **preheated** 400° oven for 15 minutes, until soft and fragrant.

In a large skillet, over medium high heat, combine and sauté for 30 seconds...	2	tablespoons	*olive oil,* heated
	2	teaspoons	*fresh garlic,* minced

Add and sauté for 2 minutes...			*roasted leek,* diced
			smoked tomato, peeled, chopped
	1	cup	*black beans,* cooked al dente

Add. . .	2	cups	*fish stock* (or canned clam juice)
	16	large	*shrimp,* peeled, deveined
	16	large	*scallops*

Bring to a boil; lower heat
and simmer stew just until
the shrimp turn white.

Quickly add. . .	8	ounces	*fresh spinach,* chopped *black pepper to taste,* freshly ground

Cook for one minute and serve. Distribute stew evenly among four soup bowls and garnish with *pine nuts.*

*Smoke tomatoes in a covered grill over <u>very</u> low charcoal heat and a few chips of wet wood of your choice (hickory, mesquite, apple, alder, etc.) for about two hours. For best storage of the tomatoes not used in this recipe, peel and chop the tomatoes before placing into a glass jar and immersing them in white wine. Store in your refrigerator for up to two weeks. Use a ziplock bag for freezer storage of up to two months.

**Toast nuts in a hot skillet, tossing them quickly so they won't burn, until a golden brown.

WARM CHOCOLATE BREAD PUDDING
with BOURBON SAUCE

You may want to complement this dessert with a glass of Grahams Vintage Port 1980.

In a medium size cake pan (10" x 12"), place. . .	1 1/2	pounds	*dry bread,* coarsely chopped
Add. . .	3 1/2	cups	*milk*
	2	cups	*sugar*
	3	large	*eggs,* beaten
	1/4	cup	*cinnamon*

'Knead' mixture until all liquid
is absorbed — it will be very wet.

In a double boiler, melt together. . .	8	ounces	*semi-sweet chocolate*
			coarsely chopped
	1	teaspoon	*vanilla extract*

Add melted chocolate to bread pudding in random dollops. As if you were making a marble cake, slightly stir to combine chocolate into the bread pudding, so there are still 'heavy' sections of chocolate throughout which are supported by the bread pudding. Bake in a **preheated** 350° oven for approximately 1 1/2 to 2 hours, until the center rises and springs back when touched lightly. Remove from oven and allow to rest 15 minutes before cutting. Serve with Bourbon Sauce.

Bourbon Sauce

In a bowl, combine and mix			
thoroughly. . .	2	large	*eggs*
	1/2	cup	*sugar*
	1/2	cup	*bourbon*
	1/2	teaspoon	*vanilla extract*

In heavy saucepan, heat			
until boiling. . .	2	cups	*heavy cream*
	1/2	cup	*sugar*

Spoon half of the hot cream into the egg mixture, stirring constantly, to temper the eggs. Return all of this mixture back to the saucepan, stirring constantly, removing from heat just before it boils. Cool immediately in an ice bath.

The best way to cool the sauce down quickly is to scrape it into a stainless steel bowl and place that bowl into a larger bowl half filled with ice water. Then stir the sauce for a minute or two to help release the heat. Strain sauce through a fine sieve.

chas

When Albert and Joni Upsher opened the Snake River Brewery in 1992, they didn't just build themselves a micro brewery. They created a dining establishment which maintains a festive, high energy in a familiar, friendly atmosphere. Albert and Joni's goal is to have high value for a reasonable, affordable price....offering their customers "a lot of bang for their buck!"

That they succeed quite well is evidenced by their large local following. The Brewery is filled most evenings with Jacksonites who like to end their day congregating with friends, enjoying wood-fired pizza, fresh pastas and salad. Visitors to Jackson who find their way to Snake River Brewery will not feel like a stranger for long in this fun, friendly place!

The Brewery is in full operation throughout the year, producing 15 different beers each year. Two or three brews are made and bottled year around for distribution in and out of Jackson. There are also seasonal brews. Heavier, darker beers are brewed in the winter; lighter, golden beers are brewed in the summer. These special brews are made for consumption on the premises.

Snake River Brewery's award-winning brews and their commitment to creating all dishes from scratch, with only the freshest of ingredients, keeps customers coming back for more, and often!

MENU FOR FOUR

Bruschetta with Tapenade,
Roasted Garlic and Onion Confit

recommended wine ~ medium-bodied shiraz with raspberry and strawberry
Buckley's Shiraz

Romaine and Spinach Salad
with Gorgonzola and Toasted Walnuts
in Balsamic Vinaigrette

recommended wine ~ dry, crisp, clean sauvignon blanc
Cakebread Sauvignon Blanc

Roasted Garlic Smoked Salmon Alfredo
with Tomato Concesse

recommended wine ~ pinot noir with light currant and berry
Saintsbury Pinot Noir

Chef Chad Vermeer

Wine pairings by The Wine Loft

BRUSCHETTA with TAPENADE, ROASTED GARLIC and ONION CONFIT

Serves 4

Be sure to make the Onion Confit the day before serving.

In a bowl, combine...	2	small	*red onion,* very thinly sliced
(Onion Confit)	3/4	cup	*rice wine vinegar*
	1	tablespoon	*dill*
	2	teaspoons	*mustard seeds*
	1/4	teaspoon	*salt*
	1/4	teaspoon	*pepper*

Allow to marinate overnight in covered container in refrigerator.

To roast garlic, slice in half, horizontally...	1	whole	*garlic bulb*
Brush with...			*olive oil*

Season with...			*paprika* *kosher salt* *black pepper,* coarsely ground

Place two halves of garlic bulb, face up in baking pan. Add a little water to pan and place in **preheated** 350° oven for about 15-20 minutes, until golden brown. Remove from oven and cool to room temperature.

In food processor, combine...	1/2	pound	*black olives,* pitted
	1/2	pound	*green olives,* pitted
(Tapenade)	1/4	cup	*capers,* drained
	2	teaspoons	*garlic,* minced
	1	ounce	*anchovy filets*
Process until smooth.			

With machine running, slowly add, to desired consistency...	1/4	cup	*olive oil*

To complete recipe, you will need...   **¹/₂**   **loaf**   *French baguette,*
$^1/_4$" slices

Just before serving, brush tops of slices with olive oil; toast in **preheated** 350° oven for 5 to 10 minutes, just until bruschetta are lightly toasted on top. To serve, arrange Bruschetta on plate with Tapenade and Onion Confit; garnish with Roasted Garlic.

ROMAINE and SPINACH SALAD
with GORGONZOLA and TOASTED WALNUTS   Serves 4

In large salad bowl, place...   **¹/₂**   **pound**   *romaine,*
torn into pieces
¹/₂   **pound**   *spinach,* stems removed

Dress with Balsamic Vinaigrette and toss well.

Portion greens onto four salad plates;
sprinkle each with portion of...   **1**   **cup**   *gorgonzola,* crumbled
¹/₂   **cup**   *toasted walnuts,*
coarsely chopped

Balsamic Vinaigrette

In mixing bowl, whisk together...   **2**   **cups**   *balsamic vinegar*
2   **cups**   *olive oil*
1   **tablespoon**   *red onion,* finely diced
1   **teaspoon**   *black pepper*
1   **pinch**   *salt*

SMOKED SALMON ALFREDO with
ROASTED GARLIC and TOMATO CONCESSE   Serves 4

This recipe will smoke up to 2 sides of salmon....you'll have plenty left over for other favorite dishes. It is a good idea to do all your preparation the day before. Bringing it all together to create the entree will take very little time.

| You will need... | 4-6 | cups | *fettuccine,* |
| | | | cooked al dente |

In large sauté pan, combine...	1	tablespoon	*olive oil*
	2	tablespoons	*roasted garlic*
Sauté until golden.			
Add...	10	ounces	*Smoked Salmon,*
			broken into pieces
Deglaze with...	$^1/_4$	cup	*dry white wine*
Reduce slightly.			

Add...	1	cup	*Alfredo Sauce*
			salt and pepper
			to taste

Reduce slightly, add fettuccine and toss together. Serve topped with **Tomato Concesse**. A variation would be to serve sauce draped over the fettuccine. Another variation is to add coarsely chopped *fresh spinach* when you toss everything together.

Roasted Garlic

In small baking pan, combine...	1	cup	*garlic cloves*
	1	tablespoon	*honey*
Sprinkle with...			*water*
			olive oil

Cover pan with foil. Roast in **preheated** 325° oven for approximately one hour, until soft. Drain. Puree in food processor. Texture should be spreadable at room temperature.

Smoked Salmon

In large baking pan, combine...	1	quart	*pale ale*
	¼	cup	*liquid smoke*
	¼	cup	*fresh lemon juice*
	2	tablespoons	*Worcestershire*
	2	tablespoons	*garlic,* minced
	1	tablespoon	*dill*
Mix well.			

Add...	1-2	sides	*whole salmon,* skinned, deboned
Allow to marinate 3 hours.			

To complete, you will need...			*dijon mustard*
			cracked pepper

Remove salmon from marinade; pat dry. Coat lightly with *dijon* and *cracked pepper.* Place on rack in baking pan. Smoke salmon in a wood oven or smoker. DON'T overcook!

Alfredo Sauce

In heavy saucepan, combine...	2	cups	*heavy cream*
	1	cup	*whole milk*
	1	teaspoon	*fresh basil,* finely chopped
	1	teaspoon	*fresh oregano* chopped
Bring to a scald.			

Add and simmer to thicken...	2	cups	*parmesan cheese*

Tomato Concesse

Mix together...	4	ripe	*roma tomatoes,* seeded, finely diced
	1	tablespoon	*fresh basil,* chopped
	1	tablespoon	*fresh parsley,* chopped
	½	teaspoon	*paprika*

chas

Celebrating its seventh year on Jackson's town square, the Snake River Grill is known for its intimate and comfortable dining rooms. Said to be Jackson's best restaurant by *The Wine Spectator,* the SRG has also been the recipient of their "Award of Excellence" for six years.

As noted by DIRONA (Distinguished Restaurants of North America), the SRG features only fresh fish, free-range veal and chicken, pizzas from their wood-burning oven, organic produce, and a wine list with over 235 selections.

The Grill's interior of lodge-pole pine walls, tapestry and leather booths, a moss-rock fireplace, and three-dimensional ceiling paintings creates an interesting and beautiful environment of warmth and comfort. In addition to a great deck with views of Snow King Mountain, the SRG has an elegant private dining room.

MENU FOR SIX

Field Greens with Citrus-Chive Vinaigrette and Crumbled Goat Cheese

recommended wine - 1999 Cakebread Sauvignon Blanc

Roasted Eggplant and Tomato Soup

Grilled King Salmon with Corn Nage

recommended wine - 1998 David Bruce Pinot Noir

Buttermilk Mashed Potatoes

Bear Lake Raspberries, Lemon and Buttermilk Pie

recommended wine - 1997 Chateau St. Michelle Late Harvest Riesling

Chef Jeff Drew
Pastry Chef Deno Marcum

Wine pairings by August Spier

FIELD GREENS with CITRUS-CHIVE VINAIGRETTE and CRUMBLED GOAT CHEESE   Serves 6

August Spier of Snake River Grill suggests a 1999 Cakebread Sauvignon Blanc, from Napa Valley, to enhance your enjoyment of this course.

For this recipe, you will need...	1	pound	*mixed greens*
	1/4	pound	*goat cheese,* crumbled

Toss greens with Citrus-Chive Vinaigrette and portion onto plates. Crumble goat cheese over top of salads. Serve.

Citrus-Chive Vinaigrette

In saucepan, over medium heat, combine...	1	cup	*fresh grapefruit juice*
	1	cup	*fresh orange juice*
	1	cup	*fresh lime juice*
Reduce by half. Cool.			

Whisk in...	2	cups	*olive oil*
Add...	2	teaspoons	*fresh chives,* finely chopped
	2	teaspoons	*orange zest,* minced

ROASTED EGGPLANT and TOMATO SOUP   Serves 6

For this recipe, you will need...	2	whole	*eggplant,* quartered
	1/2	cup	*olive oil*

Finely chop and mix together...	1	tablespoon	*fresh basil*
	1	tablespoon	*fresh marjoram*
	1	tablespoon	*fresh rosemary*
	1	tablespoon	*fresh thyme*
	1	tablespoon	*fresh sage*

Add...	1	teaspoon	*kosher salt*
	1	teaspoon	*black pepper*

Brush the eggplant quarters with *olive oil* and coat with herb mixture. Place on baking sheet in **preheated** 350° oven until golden brown, about 25 minutes. Remove from oven and cool. Scoop out all pulp.

Place eggplant pulp in stock pot,

along with...	1¹/₃	quarts	*water*
	2	cloves	*roasted garlic**
	¹/₃	cup	*tomato puree*
	1	ounce	*chipotle sauce*

Bring to a simmer.
Cook for 15 minutes.

In food processor, puree soup (with a little extra water if needed for desired consistency.). Season to taste with salt and pepper.

Spread peeled garlic cloves, lightly oiled, in baking pan; place in preheated 350° oven until golden brown, about 15 minutes.

GRILLED KING SALMON with CORN NAGE   Serves 6

August recommends a David Bruce 1998 Pinot Noir, from Santa Cruz, as a very good complement to the Salmon.

For this recipe, you will need...	6	7 ounce	**King Salmon filets,** skin and pin bones removed
			olive oil
			salt and pepper

Just before you are ready to serve, brush *salmon filets* with *olive oil* and season to taste with *salt and pepper.* Grill salmon to medium rare, over hot flame, about 2 minutes per side. Serve grilled salmon on top of Corn Nage, with **Buttermilk Mashed Potatoes**.

Corn Nage

In saucepan, combine...	1	ounce	*butter*
	1	whole	*shallot,* minced
	2	cloves	*roasted garlic**
	1	teaspoon	*coriander*
	$1/2$	teaspoon	*dried thyme*

Sauté until shallots
are translucent.

| Deglaze with... | $1/2$ | cup | *white wine* |

Reduce to almost dry.

| Add... | 3 | cups | *sweet corn* |
| | 3 | cups | *clam juice* |

Simmer for 5-8 minutes,
to cook corn.

In food professor, puree...			*cooked corn*
			(with clam juice)
Add...	1	cup	*heavy cream,* scalded

Strain through fine hole china
cap or sieve. Season
to taste with...   *salt and sugar*

*Spread peeled garlic cloves, lightly oiled, in baking pan; place in preheated 350° oven until golden brown, about 15 minutes.

BUTTERMILK MASHED POTATOES
Serves 6

| In large pot, place... | 6 | whole | *Yukon Gold potatoes* peeled |

Cover with salted water. Boil until potatoes are soft. Push potatoes through fine ricer.

Add and mix well...	3/4	cup	*buttermilk*
	1/2	cup	*butter,* melted
Season with...			*salt and pepper* *to taste*

BEAR LAKE RASPBERRIES, LEMON and BUTTERMILK PIE
Serves 6

A 1997 Chateau St. Michelle, Late Harvest Riesling would be delicious with thisbuttermilk pie.

| For this recipe, you will need... | 1 | 9 inch | *pie pan* *aluminum foil* |
| | 4 | cups | *uncooked beans, rice* *or pie weights* |

To make pie shell, in large bowl, combine...	1/2	pound	*unsalted butter,* chilled, cut up
	2	cups	*flour*
	3	tablespoons	*sugar*
	1	teaspoon	*sea salt*

Use pastry cutter to combine the ingredients until the mixture resembles coarse cornmeal with pea-sized pieces of butter throughout.

| Gently add... | 3 | tablespoons | *ice cold water* |

Stir to moisten mixture. Use your hands to bring the dough together and form it into a single ball. Wrap dough in plastic and refrigerate for 30 minutes.

After chilling, roll the dough into a circle about 1/4" thick. Transfer rolled out dough to 9" pie pan. Gently press dough into the pan, allowing the dough to hang over the edge; trim the edge to an even $1/2$" overhang all the way around. Fold this rim under and crimp with your fingers (or with the tines of a fork) all the way around pie shell. Chill in refrigerator for another 30 minutes.

Just before baking the pie shell, place foil over it and pour beans/weights over the foil. Bake pie shell in a **preheated** 350° oven until the edges begin to turn a light golden brown, about 20 minutes. Remove the beans and foil; continue baking until a light golden brown all over, about 10 minutes more. Remove from oven; allow to cool.

Into baked pie shell, scatter...	1	pint	*Bear Lake raspberries,* picked clean, brushed free of dust

In medium size bowl, mix together until smooth...	$1^1/_2$	cups	*white sugar*
	$1/_4$	teaspoon	*salt*
	4	large	*eggs*
Add and stir just until combined...	4	tablespoons	*lemon zest,* chopped
	$1/_3$	cup	*flour,* sifted
	$1/_4$	pound	*unsalted butter,* melted, cooled

In separate bowl, combine...	$1^1/_2$	cups	*buttermilk*
	3	tablespoons	*heavy cream*
	2	tablespoons	*fresh lemon juice*
	$1/_4$	teaspoon	*vanilla extract*
	1	pinch	*ground mace*

Combine the sugar-egg mixture with buttermilk mixture and whisk until smooth. Pour the batter over the berries in the baked pie shell. Bake in a **preheated** 325° oven until the batter is just set, about 35-40 minutes. Allow to cool to room temperature. Cut into 6 pieces and serve with Whipped Cream.

Whipped Cream

Combine and whip to soft peaks...	1	cup	*heavy cream*
	2	teaspoons	*white sugar*
	1	pinch	*salt*

chas

Opening its doors for the first time in the Fall of 1983, Stiegler's Restaurant and Bar offers authentic Austrian cuisine in an ambiance rich with the culture of that country. Peter Stiegler's philosophy of fine food, excellent service and good atmosphere in equally important proportions create a dining experience you wouldn't want to miss.

Classic Austrian cuisine, a combination of ethnic cooking from Hungary, Italy and Czechoslovakia, has not changed in 150 years. Although Peter still cooks with butter and sugar (a philosophy from his Mama, whose cooking is a large influence of Stiegler's menu), he tries to go with the times and cook a little lighter. Peter maintains that the quality of ingredients is the most important part of cooking.

Using taste more than exact recipes to create his dishes, Peter's recipes are all straight out of his head. "So, please adjust the amounts to your own taste buds. Don't be scared! My red cabbage tastes different every time I make it!"

MENU FOR FOUR

Warm Cauliflower and Broccoli Salad

recommended wine ~ very light, crisp German riesling
Leonard Kreusch Piesporter

Roasted Pork Filet with Bartlett Pear and Gorgonzola Soufflé

recommended wine ~ rich riesling with vanilla and spice
Bernkateler-Doctor Kabinett

Roesti Potatoes

Apfelpalatschinken

recommended wine ~ very rich dessert wine with honey and vanilla
Nittnaus Eiswein

Chef Peter Stiegler

Wine pairings by The Wine Loft

WARM CAULIFLOWER and BROCCOLI SALAD   Serves 4

In large pot, in slightly salted water, poach or steam until tender...	1	medium	*cauliflower,* broken into flowerets
	2-3	roses	*broccoli,* broken into flowerets

To prepare dressing, combine...	1/3	cup	*light olive oil*
	1/4	cup	*cider vinegar*
	1/2		*roasted red pepper,* finely diced
	1	tablespoon	*fresh chives,* finely sliced
	1	teaspoon	*caraway seeds*
	1/2	teaspoon	*garlic,* minced
			salt and pepper to taste

To complete recipe, you will need...	1	bunch	*greens,* rinsed

Toss cauliflower and broccoli with dressing and serve on small bed of *fresh greens.*

ROASTED PORK FILET with
BARTLETT PEAR and GORGONZOLA SOUFFLÉ   Serves 4

Poach the pears ahead of time and hold them at room temperature until ready. While the pork tenderloins are finishing in the oven, slice the pears to have ready for the final presentation.

Remove fat and silverskin from...	1 1/2	pounds	*pork tenderloin*
Rub on...			*fresh garlic,* minced *dijon mustard*
And season with...			*salt and pepper to taste*

In ovenproof skillet, melt and heat...	2	tablespoons	*butter*

Add, to sear on all sides...			*pork tenderloins*
Deglaze with...	¹/₂	cup	*white wine*

Place skillet in **preheated** 375° oven for 8-10 minutes. Let rest in warm place for 10 minutes before slicing. To serve, slice pork tenderloin in ¹/₂" thick slices. On baking sheet, arrange 3 slices of pork for each serving, top with slices of *poached pear* and about one tablespoon of Gorgonzola Soufflé. Place under broiler to brown. It will only take a few moments to brown...watch carefully so it doesn't burn.

Poached Bartlett Pear

In saucepan, combine...	1	cup	*water*
(simple syrup)	1	cup	*sugar*
	1	teaspoon	*fresh lemon juice*
Simmer until becomes syrup.			

Add...	2	quartered	*Bartlett pears,* peeled
Simmer gently for 10 minutes. Remove from syrup, slice ¹/₄" thick and hold warm.			

Gorgonzola Soufflé

In mixing bowl, whisk together...	¹/₄	pound	*gorgonzola cheese* soft, room temperature
	2		*egg yolks*
Whip together well.			

In different bowl, whip until stiff...	2		*egg whites*

Fold stiff egg whites into cheese and egg yolk mixture.

ROESTI POTATOES

In saucepan, parboil in water... Boil until you can poke them with a fork to about $1/2$" depth.	2	whole	*Idaho potatoes*

Grate potatoes and mix with...	1	small	*onion,* finely diced
	1	whole	*egg,* beaten *salt and pepper to taste*

Form potato mixture into one large pancake, about 9" in diameter. In medium hot skillet, sauté on both sides until golden brown. To serve, slice into 6 wedges.

APFELPALATSCHINKEN

Serves 4-6

In mixing bowl, make a batter of...	1	large	*egg*
	¹/₂	cup	*milk*
	¹/₂ cup + 1	tablespoon	*flour*
	2	tablespoons	*butter,* melted
	1	pinch	*salt*

This batter should make 4 to 6, 6" pancakes (palatschinken),which should be a little thicker than a crepe.

In saucepan, combine...	1	tablespoon	*butter,* melted
	2	large	*granny smith apples,* peeled, thinly sliced
	2	tablespoons	*white sugar*
	1	ounce	*raisins*
	1	teaspoon	*cinnamon*

Cook over medium heat until apples are soft.

| Deglaze with... | 2 | tablespoons | *dark rum* |

To complete recipe, you will need...

powdered sugar
whipped cream

Fold a large spoonful of apple filling into each palatschinken. Sprinkle with *powdered sugar.* Serve with *whipped cream.*

Just eight miles north of the town of Jackson, lies the beautiful Jackson Hole Golf and Tennis Club. There you will find the Strutting Grouse restaurant. With its magnificent views of the Grand Teton, it will be a feast for your eyes as well as your other senses. Whether dining before the stone fireplace in their cozy dining room, or out on their patio, you will enjoy excellent regional cuisine.

The Jackson Hole Golf and Tennis Club offers its guests a true country club experience, boasting a Robert Trent Jones, Jr. 18-hole championship course, rated as the best in Wyoming by Golf Digest. The golf course, six Plexicushion tennis courts, and its beautiful outdoor swimming pool are all open to the public.

As a part of the Grand Teton Lodge Company, the Strutting Grouse is fortunate to have Executive Chef Joe Santangini create its menu and recipes. While overseeing three restaurants at the lodges and resorts of GTLC in Grand Teton National Park, he has graciously prepared a few of his recipes for us!

MENU FOR SIX

Beef Consommé

Avocado, Orange and Pear Salad
with Sesame Orange Dressing

recommended wine ~ dry, crisp sauvignon blanc with light pineapple
Murphy-Goode Fume Blanc

Fillet du Boeuf Florentine

recommended wine ~ bold merlot with dark blackberry
Raymond Napa Valley Merlot

Strutter's Chocolate Mousse

recommended wine ~ light, mildly sweet aperitif with melon and honey
Lillet

Chef Joseph Santangini

Wine pairings by The Wine Loft

BEEF CONSOMMÉ

Serves 10

In food processor, chop...	2 3/8	ounces	*celery,* trimmed
(mirepoix)	2 3/8	ounces	*onions,* peeled
	1 5/8	ounces	*carrots,* peeled

Add...	1 5/8	cups	*egg whites*
	1	ounce	*tomato paste*
	22	whole	*black peppercorns,* crushed
	3/4	ounce	*beef silverskin*
	1/4	pound	*beef,* coarsely ground
Blend together. This mixture is called *raft.*			

In large stockpot, combine...	9 5/8	cups	*veal stock,** cold *raft*

Stir well. Bring slowly to simmer, stirring often until boiling begins on side of pot. Do not stir again. Let raft form on top. Simmer until raft is fully cooked and stock is clear, about 2 hours. Strain stock carefully through fine china cap or sieve with cheese cloth. Be sure to drain completely. Allow consommé to cool completely before refrigerating (covered) until use. To serve, reheat over low heat and bring just to a simmer.

For richness of the soup, the quality of the stock is important. Canned stock can be substituted. but it won't be the same. Homemade chicken stock would be a preferable substitute. Veal stock is basically the same as beef stock, except made with veal bones; see index for recipes.

AVOCADO, ORANGE and PEAR SALAD
with SESAME ORANGE DRESSING
Serves 6

This salad was featured at the 1995 Food and Wine Classic!

Just before serving, in large salad bowl, toss together...	1 whole	*avocado,* peeled, minced
	3 whole	*navel oranges,* peeled, diced (core discarded)
	2 whole	*pears,* peeled, diced (core discarded)
	1/2 cup	*green onions,* minced
	1/4 cup	*fresh basil,* julienned
	1/4 cup	*fresh mint,* julienned
	1 bunch	*watercress,* stems removed
		Sesame Orange Dressing
Sprinkle with...	2 tablespoons	*black sesame seeds*

Sesame Orange Dressing

In food processor, combine...	1 1/2 cups	*orange juice*
	1 cup	*rice wine vinegar*
	1 tablespoon	*shallot,* minced
	1 tablespoon	*garlic,* minced
	1/2 tablespoon	*ginger root,* peeled, minced
Add...	2 tablespoons	*sesame seeds*
	1/2 cup	*sesame oil*
		salt and pepper to taste
With machine running, slowly drizzle in until desired consistency...	3 cups	*canola oil*

FILLET du BOEUF FLORENTINE

Serves 6

For this recipe, you will need...	3	pounds	*beef tenderloin,* (whole)

In sauté pan, over medium heat, combine...

	2	tablespoons	*butter*
	1¼	pounds	*fresh spinach*

Sauté until spinach is limp. Drain well.

In mixing bowl, combine...

			cooked spinach
	2³⁄₈	ounces	*fresh basil,* chopped
	3⁵⁄₈	ounces	*parmesan cheese,* freshly grated
	2	large	*egg yolks*
	1	tablespoon	*garlic,* minced
	1	tablespoon	*shallots,* minced

Create a pocket in *beef tenderloin* by inserting a knife from both ends towards the center. Use cook's steel to enlarge the pocket. Stuff pocket until filled with spinach mixture. Season outside of tenderloin with salt and pepper.

In hot skillet, sear tenderloin on all sides. Bake in **preheated** 350° oven for 30 minutes, or until internal temperature reaches 115°. Let rest 10-15 minutes. Slice and serve.

STRUTTER'S CHOCOLATE MOUSSE

Serves 6

In top of double boiler, combine...	9	ounces	*semi-sweet chocolate*
	3	tablespoons	*water*
Stir until chocolate is melted.			

In mixing bowl, beat until lemon colored...	6	large	*egg yolks*
With a whisk, slowly drizzling the hot, melted chocolate, gradually beat the chocolate into the yolks.			
Blend in...	1	tablespoon	*vanilla extract*

In another bowl, whip until stiff...	6	large	*egg whites*
Fold into chocolate mixture.			

In another bowl, whip until stiff...	1 $\frac{1}{8}$	cups	*heavy cream*
Fold $2/3$ of the whipped cream into chocolate mixture.			

Fold in...	1 $\frac{1}{2}$	ounces	*semi-sweet chocolate,* grated

Pipe mousse into glass stemware or other attractive glassware. Chill, covered, until ready to serve. Garnish top with dollops of remaining third of *whipped cream,* sweetened slightly.

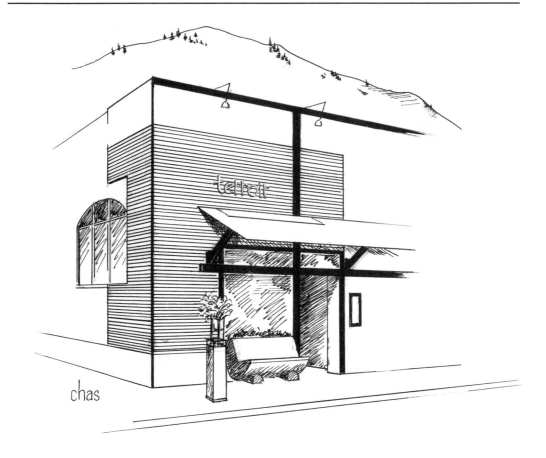

chas

In February of 1999, Restaurant Terroir opened in Jackson Hole. Within a year of opening, owners Ben Roth and Ken Fredrickson received recognition from *Food and Wine*, *Usa Today*, *New York Times*, *Wine Spectator*, and the *La Times*, in addition to local accolades.

Terroir, which is pronounced as "tair-wahr," is a French term meaning the essence of a vineyard site or region encompassing soil, climate, sunlight. It is an expression of the earth. With this translation, Restaurant Terroir possesses a rustic, yet contemporary and comfortable ambiance, also reflective of the mountainous environment of Jackson Hole. It's beautiful!

Featuring a French bistro fare with global influences, ranging from steaming mussels to rack of lamb, Terroir's menu is guided by the seasons and the expertise of renowned chef and partner Scott Sampson. Master Sommelier Ken Fredrickson has developed one of the most extensive wine lists in the valley, featuring more than 200 selections stored in a temperature-controlled, custom wine cellar visible from the dining room.

In combination with Terroir's focus on the four elements of dining....ambiance, food, service, and wine....it is obvious that Restaurant Terroir has taken dining to another dimension in Jackson Hole.

MENU FOR EIGHT

Belgium Endive with Apples, Walnuts, Roquefort and Champagne Vinaigrette

recommended wine ~ dry, light-bodied white burgandy
Boyer-Martenot Meursault

Seared Alaskan Halibut with Corn/Morel Flan and Summer Pea Veloute

recommended wine ~ white bordeaux with lemon and light grapefruit
Mouton Cadet

Creme Brulee

recommended wine ~ French dessert wine thick with honey, clean smooth finish
Chapoutier Muscat

Chef du Cuisine
Scott R. Sampson

Wine pairings by The Wine Loft

BELGIUM ENDIVE with APPLES, WALNUTS, ROQUEFORT and CHAMPAGNE VINAIGRETTE   Serves 8

Cut out heart, rinse and drain well... Chill.	8 heads	*Belgium endive*
In large bowl, combine...	2 whole	*Granny Smith apples,* sliced*
	1/2 cup	*walnuts,* chopped
	1/2 cup	*Roquefort,* crumbled
Drizzle with...		*Champagne Vinaigrette*

Toss well. Adjust seasoning with salt and pepper if necessary.

If preparing ahead, dip apple slices in a lemon-water bath to prevent them from turning brown.

Champagne Vinaigrette

Whisk together...	1 1/2 cups	*walnut oil*
	1/2 cup	*champagne vinegar*
		salt and pepper to taste

Blend for 2 minutes to emulsify vinaigrette.

SEARED ALASKAN HALIBUT with
CORN /MOREL FLAN and SUMMER VELOUTE   Serves 8

This is a great recipe for entertaining, especially in the summer when corn is at its peak. You can do all your preparation ahead of time, leaving about 15 minutes to cook the halibut and bring it all together.

For this recipe you will need...	8	6-8 ounce	*Alaskan Halibut filets,* 1" thick
			clarified butter
			kosher salt
			pepper, fresh ground

Season halibut filets with kosher salt and pepper to taste. Sear halibut filets in clarified butter in an extremely hot skillet, approximately 1-2 minutes on each side. Keep warm. To serve, place seared Alaskan halibut on plate along with **Corn/Morel Flan**, and drape with **Summer Pea Veloute.**

Corn/Morel Flan

If using dried morels, rehydrate them in warm water and drain well before slicing.

In sauté pan, over medium heat, combine...	3	tablespoons	*whole butter*
	1	tablespoon	*shallots,* minced
Sauté until shallots are translucent.			

Add...	8	large	*morel mushrooms,* thoroughly cleaned and thinly sliced
Cook until morels are tender, approximately 2 minutes.			
Season with...			*salt and pepper*
Cool.			

In pot of cold water, place...	2	small	*fresh corn on cob*
	1	teaspoon	*salt*
Bring to a boil; remove corn.			
Cool. Cut corn off cob.			

In bowl, combine...	8	large	*eggs,* beaten
	¹⁄₂	cup	*milk*
	¹⁄₂	cup	*heavy cream*
	2	tablespoons	*chives,* finely chopped
			salt and pepper
			to taste

Beat well.

Fold cooked and cooled corn and morel mushrooms into custard mixture. Portion out into eight 4 oz. ramekins which have been oiled or buttered to prevent sticking. Place ramekins in water bath [i.e. large baking pan carefully filled with water until water level is halfway up side of ramekins] Bake in **preheated** 325° oven for one hour, until set. Remove ramekins from water bath and hold at room temperature.

To serve, run a thin knife around the inside of the ramekin to loosen the flan. Invert the ramekin and gently place the flan on plate atop the **Summer Pea Veloute**.

Summer Pea Veloute

Be sure to clean leeks well, under running water, before chopping.

In sauté pan, over **low** heat, combine...	2	large	*leeks* (white part only), chopped
	2	tablespoons	*butter*
Sauté until leeks are tender and translucent.			

Add...	1	cup	*chicken stock*
Bring to a boil and add...	2	teaspoons	*roux*
Gently simmer over low heat for 15 mintues.			

[**Roux** is made by melting butter, adding an equal portion of flour, then cooking, while stirring constantly, over medium heat for 1-2 minutes]

| Add... | 8 | whole | *sugar snap peas* |

Continue simmering veloute just until peas are tender, keeping their bright green color. Using a blender or emulsion blender, puree mixture and then strain through fine sieve into shallow saucepan.

To finish sauce, fold in...	4	tablespoons	*heavy cream*
	4	tablespoons	*butter.* softened
			white pepper and
			salt to taste

Heat just to serving temperature.

A really nice touch when serving is to garnish the top of the flan with deep fried **julienne of leeks,** piled high. To accomplish this, julienne the white part of leek, dust with cornstarch and deep fry very quickly in very hot oil. Remove from oil and drain on papertowels until ready to use.

CREME BRULEE

This is a signature dish at Terroir. It is one of the very best creme brulees I've ever tasted!

In heavy saucepan, scald...	$4\,^1/_3$	cups	*heavy cream*
	2	whole	*bourbon vanilla*
			beans,* split

Before discarding vanilla beans,
scrape seeds from beans into milk

| In mixing bowl, beat together... | 15 | large | *egg yolks* |
| | $1^1/_8$ | cups | *sugar* |

Slowly whisk just $^1/_4$ cup of <u>warm</u> cream into mixture to temper egg yolks. Slowly add the rest of the cream, whisking all the while. Strain mixture through fine sieve. Ladle custard into 5 oz. ceramic ramekins. Place ramekins in water bath [large baking pan carefully filled with water halfway up side of ramekins]. Bake in preheated 325° oven until done.

Terroir uses deep ramekins to create their creme brulees, which necessitates baking them for 3 hours. If you use shallow ramekins, you will need to bake them for about 1 $^1/_2$ hours. Test the custards by shaking the ramekins. If they are done, the edges will be set and firm, and you will be able to see just a *tiny* bit of movement in center.

Remove ramekins from water bath and cool in refrigerator for two hours before serving. Just before serving, sprinkle the top of each custard with *2 tablespoons white sugar* and burn with a torch.**

Terroir uses bourbon vanilla beans; however, any type of vanilla bean can be used.
**Culinary torches are available in most kitchen/culinary stores or catalogs.*

chas

Nestled against the majestic Tetons, just minutes from downtown Jackson, the Teton Pines Golf Club boasts a beautiful 22,000 square-foot club house, surrounded by the 360-acre Arnold Palmer Golf Course, the John Gardiner Tennis Center, Jack Dennis' Fly Fishing School and a 10km cross country skiing track.

As a centerpiece of this planned development, the Teton Pines clubhouse offers fine dining in an elegant atmosphere that provides magnificent views through floor to ceiling windows. For summer dining, patrons can enjoy their meals on the outdoor terrace overlooking the golf course.

Teton Pines serves lunch and dinner, and offers private catering all year around, featuring regional American cuisine. During the summer, a country breakfast is served on Sundays. Their very talented chef, Michael Gallivan, offers the finest seafood, specially aged meats and game, as well as pasta, fresh baked breads and desserts. Chef Michael takes full advantage of the freshest of ingredients from around the world to offer a creative menu to tempt and please every guest.

MENU FOR SIX

Tequila Spiked Prawns with White Corn Pancakes

recommended wine - crisp, dry pinot gris with pear and lemongrass
Zenato Pinot Grigio

Gazpacho

recommended wine - zesty citrus sauvignon blanc with herbal hints
Celestin Blondeau Sancere

Smoked Duck Salad with Maple Raspberry Vinaigrette

recommended wine - fruitful pinot noir with cherry and light plum
"J" Pinot Noir

Artic Char with Red Thai Curry Lobster Sauce

recommended wine - rich merlot with cassis, light chocolate and blackberry
Duckhorn Merlot

Bacon-Chive Mashed Potatoes

Chef Michael Gallivan
Wine pairings by The Wine Loft

TEQUILA SPIKED PRAWNS

Serves 6

For this recipe, you will need...	18	U-10	*prawns,* peeled, deveined
In sauté pan, over low heat, rehydrate in small amount of oil...	2	whole	*dried chipotle peppers*
In large bowl, combine...	1	cup	*tequila*
	2	teaspoons	*cumin*
(marinade)	8	teaspoons	*fresh cilantro,* finely chopped
	2	teaspoons	*fresh garlic,* finely chopped
	1	teaspoon	*chili powder*
	4	ounces	*olive oil*
	8	whole	*limes,* zest only (reserve limes for juice)
	1/2	cup	*sugar*

Place peeled and deveined prawns in *marinade* for 1-2 hours or overnight. Place on grill or barbecue and squeeze *lime juice* over the top of prawns. Cook shrimp until they have just turned white. Remove from heat immediately. Serve three prawns per person, on a **White Corn Pancake** with Cilantro Sour Cream and chopped fresh tomatoes.

White Corn Pancakes

In food processor, combine...	8	ounces	*white corn polenta meal*
	1	whole	*apple,* seeded, coarsely chopped
	4	whole	*shallots,* chopped
	2	whole	*eggs*
	1	cup	*heavy cream*
	1	cup	*flour*
	1/2	cup	*sugar*
	1	tablespoon	*salt*
	1/2	teaspoon	*baking powder*

$1/2$	teaspoon	*black pepper*
1	teaspoon	*cumin*
1	teaspoon	*chili powder*

Process until all big
chunks are gone.

Fold in...	2	cups	*fresh corn,* cooked, cut from cob

Cook on griddle or in fry pan just like a pancake.

Cilantro Sour Cream

In small bowl, combine...	1	cup	*sour cream*
	2	tablespoons	*fresh cilantro,* chopped
Serve with additional condiment of...	3	whole	*roma tomatoes,* chopped

GAZPACHO

Serves 6

In blender or food processor, combine...	1	clove	*garlic,* crushed
	$1/2$	small bottle	*Wishbone Italian Dressing*

Blend well.

In large bowl, combine...			*dressing blended with garlic*
	$1/2$	small bottle	*Wishbone Italian Dressing*
	24	ounces	*tomato juice*
	1	large can	*crushed tomatoes*
	1	whole	*cucumber,* peeled, seeded, diced
	1	whole	*green pepper,* seeded, diced

1	whole	*yellow onion,* diced
1	small can	*pimientos,* diced
2	tablespoons	*parsley,* finely chopped*
		salt and pepper to taste

To serve, ladle into well-chilled
bowls and garnish with...

cucumber sticks
croutons
sour cream

So that the parsley color won't bleed into the gazpacho, squeeze the parsley dry in a cloth or paper towel before adding to soup.

SMOKED DUCK SALAD
Serves 6

In large salad bowl, combine...		
3/4	pound	*smoked duck,* thinly sliced
3	ounces	*Cambazola* (blue goat cheese)
3	ounces	*walnuts,* toasted*
3/4	ounce	*cracklins*
2	whole	*blood oranges,* sliced
3/4	pound	*field greens*
6	ounces	*Maple Raspberry Vinaigrette*
		salt and pepper to taste

Serve on salad plates and top
with equal portions of...

3	ounces	*red delicious apples,* sliced, oven dried

**Toast nuts in a hot skillet. Toss them quickly and do not let them burn.*

Maple Raspberry Vinaigrette

In electric mixer, combine...	$1/2$	cup	*pure maple syrup*
	$1/4$	cup	*dijon mustard*
Blend well.			

With machine running, slowly add...	1	cup	*olive oil*
	1	cup	*vegetable oil*
	1	cup	*raspberry vinegar*
	$1/2$	cup	*pure maple syrup*
Blend until well emulsified.			

Add...	$1/4$	cup	*dried tarragon leaves*
	$3/4$	teaspoon	*salt*
Mix for additional 10 minutes.			

Store in glass container at room temperature. It will separate; just whip with wire whisk to re-emulsify.

ARCTIC CHAR
with RED THAI CURRY LOBSTER SAUCE   Serves 6

| For this recipe, you will need... | 2 | pounds | *Arctic Char,* cut into 6 ounce portions clarified butter* |

| Season char with... | | | *salt and pepper to taste* |

In sauté pan, heat *clarified butter* until almost smoking. Place char skin side down and let sear, approximately 2 minutes. Turn over and gently remove skin [reserve]. Let char finish cooking, approximately 4 minutes. Cut reserved char skin into small diamond shapes to use as garnish.

To serve, place spoonful of Bacon-Chive Mashed Potatoes in middle of dinner plate, ladle Red Thai Curry Lobster Sauce around potatoes, place char on top of potatoes. Sprinkle 'diamonds' of char skin around plate.

Arctic Char is a farm raised, fresh water trout, which resembles a Brook trout in markings and comes from cold water climates.

Red Thai Curry Lobster Sauce

In sauté pan, combine...	2	teaspoons	*clarified butter*
	1	small	*onion,* finely diced
	1	stalk	*celery,* finely diced
	1	medium	*carrot,* finely diced
Cook over medium heat until vegetables are soft.			

Add...	2	cups	*water*
	1	tablespoon	*lobster base**
	2	quarts	*heavy cream*
Reduce by half. Strain sauce through fine sieve.			

To complete recipe, you will need...	1	tablespoon	*Red Thai curry paste**

To add curry paste, thin first with a little water; then add to the cream sauce. Check flavor and add salt to taste.

Available in specialty sections of grocers/catalogs. See Spice Merchant (Participating Restaurants Index, page v).

BACON-CHIVE MASHED POTATOES   Serves 6

For this recipe, you will need...   5   **pounds**   *baking potatoes*
                                    1¹/₄   **pounds**   *butter*

Boil *potatoes*, remove from heat and let sit in water for a few minutes. Drain and combine with *butter* in mixer. Salt and pepper to taste.

These are traditional French mashed potatoes. They can be made with less butter, substituting water or chicken broth.

Just before serving, fold into potatoes...   *crisp cooked bacon,*
                                                                crumbled
                                                         fresh chives, finely
                                                                chopped or snipped

PART II

Selected Recipes Restaurants

WILD MUSHROOM and ASPARAGUS RISOTTO
with GRILLED DUCK SAUSAGE

Serves 8

Use dried mushrooms and rehydrate them in hot water before slicing; incorporate this water into your stock when cooking the risotto, for added flavor.

For this recipe, you will need...	2	quarts	*chicken stock,* heated to a simmer

In saucepot, heat...	2	tablespoons	*olive oil*
Add...	1	small	*onion,* diced small
Cook over medium heat until translucent. Stir in...	1	pound	*arborio rice*

Add...	1/3	of	*chicken stock*

Stir and cook slowly until stock is absorbed. Add another third of stock and repeat. Do this again until all stock is incorporated and the rice is somewhat creamy, yet fully cooked*(risotto)*. Remove from heat and set aside.

In large sauté pan, combine...	2	tablespoons	*olive oil,* heated
	2	large	*garlic cloves,* minced
	2	ounces	*shitake mushrooms,* (dried) sliced
	2	ounces	*chanterelle mushrooms,* (dried) sliced
	2	ounces	*morel mushrooms,* (dried) sliced

| | 1 | pound | *asparagus,* washed, cut in small pieces |

Cook until vegetables are tender. Deglaze pan with...

| | 1/4 | cup | *dry white wine* |

Cook for 2 minutes. Add the *risotto* and stir well to incorporate. Season with *salt and pepper* to your discretion. The risotto should be loose and a little wet. A small amount of cream may be added if desired.

To complete recipe, you will need...

| | 8 | 4 ounce | *duck sausages* |
| | 1/2 | cup | *asiago cheese* |

Grill *duck sausages* on a very hot grill until the skin is blistered and juices appear, about 10 minutes. Slice the sausage at an angle to be placed on the risotto.

To serve, place the finished risotto in a bowl or on a plate, arrange the sliced sausage on the dish. Sprinkle with the *asiago cheese* and serve with good bread.

Beantown
CAFE & COFFEE HOUSE

APPLE DAPPLE CAKE
by Karen Raynes

In mixer, combine and mix well...	3	whole	*eggs*
	2	cups	*brown sugar*
	1	cup	*vegetable oil*
	2	teaspoons	*vanilla*

In separate bowl, blend together...	2	cups	*unbleached flour*
	1	teaspoon	*cinnamon*
	1	teaspoon	*baking soda*
	1	teaspoon	*salt*

Add this flour mixture to egg sugar mixture and mix well.

Add and mix well...	1	cup	*shredded coconut*
	1	cup	*pecans,* finely chopped
	3	cups	*granny smith apples,* peeled, seeded, diced

Pour batter into greased cake pan. Bake in **preheated** 350° oven for 45-60 minutes, until a toothpick inserted in middle comes out clean. Fresh from oven, while cake is still hot in pan, poke cake all over the top with fork. Immediately pour **Glaze** evenly over entire cake, making sure to get all the edges so the glaze will seep down the sides.

Glaze

In saucepan, combine...	1/2	cup	*brown sugar*
	1/4	cup	*butter*
	2	tablespoons	*milk*

Bring to boil, then simmer for 4 minutes. Pour over cake immediately, while glaze and cake are still hot.

Betty Rock is a wonderful cafe on Pearl Street where you can enjoy scrumptious baked goods and cappuccino, along with fabulous salads, paninis, wraps, and soup for lunch or early supper. They bake all their sweets on premise, including their own foccacio bread. Betty Rock is one of my favorite spots for lunch or for enjoying a quick dinner.

CINNAMON ROLLS

Betty Rock makes their cinnamon rolls in huge batches. Here is the recipe you can make at home!

In large mixing bowl with dough hook, put...	1 ½	cups	*water,* warmed to 105°
	2	tablespoons	*yeast*
	½ cup + 3	tablespoons	*sugar*
Let alone until it bubbles			

Add to mixture...	7	tablespoons	*butter,* softened
	1	cup	*milk*
	7	whole	*eggs*
	2	teaspoons	*salt*
	1 ½	teaspoons	*vanilla*
	½ cup + 3	tablespoons	*wheat bran*
	7	cups	*unbleached white flour*
Mix together, then add until desired consistency...	1-2	add'l cups	*flour*

Dough should be firm but light in texture. Place dough in large bowl, cover with two layers of plastic wrap, sealed well. Let rise 24 hours in refrigerator.

Combine together and microwave for 4 mintues...	$1/3$	pound	*butter*
	2	cups	*brown sugar*

Stir in until mixture is dark brown...	1-2	tablespoons	*cinnamon*
Optional ingredients...	$1/2$	cup	*walnuts or pecans,* chopped
	$1/2$	cup	*raisins*

In mixer, combine...	$1/2$	cup	*powdered sugar*
	$1/4$	cup	*water*

Whip until all lumps are gone to make simple *icing*.

To form cinnamon rolls: roll dough out into a large flat rectangle $1/8$" to $1/4$" thick. Spread butter mixture evenly onto dough, all the way to the edges. Sprinkle nuts and raisins over dough. Roll up dough, lengthwise, and cut into $2\,1/2$" pieces. Place on baking sheet, covered with parchment paper, three inches apart. Brush with **egg wash**. Bake in **preheated** 325° oven for 20-25 minutes, until golden and firm.

While cinnamon rolls are still slightly warm, spread with *icing*.

SOUR CREAM COFFEE CAKE

In mixing bowl, cream together...	1	cup	*butter*
	$1\,1/4$	cups	*sugar*

Add...	2	whole	*eggs*
	1	cup	*sour cream*
	1	teaspoon	*vanilla*

Combine and then add...	3	cups	*flour*
	$1/2$	teaspoon	*soda*
	1	teaspoon	*baking powder*

To complete recipe, you will need...   **1 ¹/₂   cups**   *berries of choice*

Butter or grease springform pan. Pour batter into pan and top with blueberries, blackberries or raspberries. Bake in **preheated** 325° oven for one hour. Sprinkle generously with **Streusel**. Put back in oven and bake until cake pulls away from sides of pan, approximately 30 minutes more.

Streusel

In mixing bowl, combine...

³/₄	cup	*oats*
³/₄	cup	*almonds,* sliced
¹/₂	cup	*cake flour*
¹/₂	cup	*white sugar*
¹/₂	cup	*brown sugar*
1	teaspoon	*cinnamon*
¹/₂	teaspoon	*nutmeg*

Add...   **about ¹/₂   cup**   *butter,* softened

Mix in enough butter until crumbly, to make pea-sized crumbs

Maple Pecan Streusel

In mixing bowl, combine...

1	cup	*oats*
1	cup	*brown sugar*
¹/₂	cup	*cake flour*
1	cup	*pecans*

Add...   **about ¹/₄   cup**   *pure maple syrup*
   ¹/₄   cup   *butter,* softened

Mix in equal parts of maple syrup and butter until crumbly.

THAI CHICKEN WRAP

*The secret of this delicious wrap is the **Thai Peanut Sauce** and the chicken marinade. With the sauce recipe, you will have enough for another meal. Betty Rock's suggestion is to mix the sauce with noodles, chicken, fresh cilantro and ground peanuts. Yum!*

In a mixing bowl, combine...	1/2	cup	*soy sauce*
	1/4	cup	*mustard*
(marinade)	1	tablespoon	*fresh ginger,* finely chopped
	1	tablespoon	*garlic,* minced
	1/4	cup	*vegetable oil*

Into marinade, place...	2	whole	*chicken breasts,* boneless, skinless

Marinate chicken for at least one hour. Grill or bake chicken until done. Slice thinly.

To complete recipe, you will need...	4	large	*spinach tortillas,* preferably 12"
	1/4 to 1/2	head	*purple cabbage,* chopped
	1	small	*cucumber,* peeled, chopped
	1	whole	*green onion,* chopped
	8	sprigs	*fresh cilantro,* chopped

On tortilla, spread 2-3 tablespoons Thai Peanut Sauce; top with chicken slices. Add small handfuls of *purple cabbage, cucumbers, onion* and *cilantro*. Fold two opposite sides of tortilla in over the ingredients; then starting with one of the other sides, roll the tortilla 'burrito' fashion as tightly as possible. Slice in half and serve.

Thai Peanut Sauce

In sauté pan, over medium heat, combine...	1	tablespoon	*peanut oil*
	3-4	tablespoons	*fresh ginger,* grated
	4	tablespoons	*garlic,* minced
	3	tablespoons	*fish sauce*
Cook for one minute.			

Add...	1	cup	*prunes,* pitted
	8	tablespoons	*Panang red curry paste*
	2	14 oz. cans	*coconut milk*
	$1/2$	cup	*brown sugar*
	$1/3$	cup	*peanut butter*
	2	teaspoons	*red pepper flakes*
Simmer one minute and add...	1	cup	*water*

Transfer mixture to food processor and add...	$1\,1/2$	tablespoons	*curry powder*
	$3/4$	tablespoon	*tumeric*
	2	tablespoons	*lemon juice*
	$1\,1/2$	tablespoons	*rice wine vinegar*

Puree to blend well.

Here are three great recipes from a brand new express 'cafe' in downtown Jackson. Owned by Tish Banta Davies, previous owner of the famous Rocky Mountain Oyster in Teton Village (and a good friend who helped me get the Cafe started years ago!), the Downtowner offers espresso, delicious baked goods, paninis, grilled sandwiches and wonderful soups.

RED BEANS and RICE SOUP
with CAJUN SAUSAGE

In large stockpot combine...	$1/2$	pound	*margarine*
	4	large	*onions,* chopped
	1	bunch	*celery,* chopped
	2	small	*carrots,* diced
	1	whole	*green pepper,* seeded, diced
Sauté until onions are translucent.			

Add...	1	gallon	*water*
	3	slices	*bacon,* chopped
	$3/4$	cup	*chicken base*
	2	tablespoons	*garlic powder*
	$1/4$	cup	*black pepper*
	$1/2$	cup	*parsley,* chopped
	3	cups	*red beans,* rinsed
Bring to a boil. Reduce to a simmer until beans are cooked, about $1^{1}/_{2}$ hours. As beans cook, add water as needed.			

Add...	$1^{1}/_{4}$	cups	*white rice*
	$1^{3}/_{4}$	pounds	*cajun sausage,* diced
Cook for another 20 minutes.			

Add....	1/4	cup	*jalapenos,* diced
	1/4	cup	*file* (spice)
			tabasco to taste

Simmer another 10 minutes. Serve.

TOMATO CHEDDAR BISQUE

In food processor, puree...	4	large	*onions*
	1/2	bunch	*celery*
	4	medium	*carrots*
Place in stockpot with...	1/2	cup	*margarine*
Sauté until vegetables are tender.			

In food processor, puree...	3	quarts	*diced tomatoes*
Add to stockpot with...	1	46 oz can	*tomato juice*
	1/2	cup	*chicken base*
	1/4	cup	*parsley,* chopped
	2	tablespoons	*black pepper*
Cook until heated completely.			

Add...	1	can	*beer of choice*
	2	cups	*cheddar cheese,* grated
Stir to fully incorporate.			
Add...	2	cups	*heavy cream*

PUMPKIN CHOCOLATE CHIP MUFFINS

In large mixing bowl, combine...	3½	cups	*unbleached flour*
	2½	cups	*sugar*
	3	teaspoons	*baking soda*
	1½	teaspoons	*cinnamon*
	1	teaspoon	*nutmeg*
Stir together.			

Add...	4	whole	*eggs*
	1	cup	*vegetable oil*
	²/₃	cup	*water*
	2	cups	*pumpkin*
Mix well.			
Stir in...	2	cups	*chocolate chips*

Pour batter into lined muffin tins, ³/₄ full. Bake in **preheated** 375° oven for 25 to 30 minutes, until toothpick inserted in center of muffin comes out clean. Remove from oven and allow to cool.

Grateful Bread is a cozy bakery which features wonderful breads of many varieties and flavors. Though grocery stores and several restaurants in the valley carry their breads, I prefer to visit the source and enjoy the fantastic aromas escaping from the ovens! Grateful Bread's specialties include a nine-grain sandwich bread; a sweet, dense Sunny French loaf; and both a spinach-parmesan and a robust garlic sourdough. Owners Betsy Van Horn and Thea Sacks are graciously sharing two of their other favorites with us.

PESTO BOWLS   Makes 2 loaves

In mixer, with dough hook,
    combine...

2	cups	*hot water*
$^1/_4$ cup + 2	tablespoons	*olive oil*
2	tablespoons	*sugar*
2	tablespoons	*salt*
$^1/_4$	cup	*yeast*
2	cups	*flour*

    Mix for about 5 minutes,
    until smooth.

Add...

$^1/_4$ cup + 2	tablespoons	*parmesan,* grated
$^1/_4$ cup + 2	tablespoons	*garlic,* minced
$^1/_4$ cup + 2	tablespoons	*dried basil,* crushed

    Finish with...   additional   *flour*

Dough is finished and ready to be removed from mixer when it has gathered onto the dough hook and cleaned itself from the sides of the bowl.

Place dough into a covered container, in a warm place. Let double in size. Punch it down and allow to double again.

Remove dough and cut in half. Hand form into two balls. Again place formed dough into covered containers (each with room to double) in a warm place. Allow to double in size. Remove and place on a large baking sheet. Place in **preheated** 350° oven and bake for approximately 30 minutes. Halfway through baking, brush with olive oil. Bowls are baked when they turn a dark golden brown, and tapping the bottom results in a drum-like sound.

SUNFLOWER BERRY BREAD   Makes 2 loaves

In mixer, with dough hook,
   combine...

2	cups	*water,* 105°
2	tablespoons	*canola oil*
2	tablespoons	*white sugar*
1	tablespoon	*salt*
1/4	cup	*yeast*
2	cups	*flour* (white, high gluten)

Mix for about 5 minutes,
until smooth.

Add...

1/2	cup	*honey*
1 1/4	cups	*blueberries**
1/3	cup	*sunflower seeds*

Finish with...   additional   *flour*

Dough is finished and ready to be removed from mixer when it has gathered onto the dough hook and cleaned itself from the sides of the bowl. The texture of the dough should be spongy. If it has more of a putty-feeling, add pinches of sugar and mix until it feels spongy. Place finished dough in covered container, in warm place. Let dough double in size. Punch it down. Again, let it double.

Remove dough and cut in half. Fold into forms. Place into greased loaf pans. Proof for about 30 minutes, until double in size, in very moist 98° proof box. For those of us without proof boxes, set loaves in warm, steamy bathroom to proof!

Bake in **preheated** 325° oven until sides of loaves are medium brown and when lifted out of pans and tapped on bottom, the bread sounds hollow.

*If using frozen blueberries, allow berries to thaw. Drain well before incorporating them into dough.

KOSHU

W I N E   B A R

Owned by Master Sommelier Ken Fredrickson, on site in his Jackson Hole Wine Company, it is not surprising that Koshu boasts a wine list of over 800 selections. Their very progressive 'wines by the glass' are tasted by the staff daily to insure wine recommendations are well matched to the customer's dinner choices. Ken has included his wine recommendations for each of the recipes Koshu shares with us here!

Very contemporary in design and venue, Koshu 's Chef, Joel Holland, delights his guests with Asian fusion food. Described by Joel as a blending of East and West; classic, traditional cuisine with a twist, using French techniques with Asian ingredients. The result is superb! With a constantly changing menu, guests may enjoy Thai, Japanese, French or Chinese cuisine, all with a 'twist'. A good example is Rack of Lamb with a Blue Cheese Miso Sauce.

MISO SOUP
with ENOKI MUSHROOM GARNISH   Serves 4

In large saucepan, combine...	1	quart	*water*
	1	2" x 4" piece	*kombu**
	1	small handful	*bonito flakes**

Heat just to simmering.
Remove from heat.

Strain stock and thoroughly mix in...	3	ounces	*miso paste*
Strain again.			

To complete recipe, you will need...   *firm tofu,* diced small
                                                    scallions, thinly sliced
                                                    enoki mushrooms

Ladle miso broth into small bowls or cups. Add diced *tofu* to each serving and garnish with *sliced scallion* and *enoki mushrooms.*

*Available in gourmond sections of grocers, culinary stores and catalogs (see Spice Merchant listed with Restaurant Addresses.

"First course usually requires a first course wine. Try something neutral which will allow the flavorful miso to be highlighted. My first choice might be an Italian Pinot Grigio. From a cool climate, it is fresh and crisp, but still very neutral. Oregon Pinot Gris would work as well. Also, keep in mind a German Riesling with a touch of sweetness would work great also."

K.L.F., Master Sommelier

WHOLE FRIED CATFISH
with CITRUS DIPPING SAUCE   Seves 4

Trout or snapper can be substituted in this recipe.

For this recipe, you will need...	1	1^1/$_2$ pound	*catfish*
	8-10	thin slivers	*fresh ginger*
			salt
			black pepper,
			freshly ground
			cornstarch
	^{1}/$_2$	bunch	*watercress*

Lay catfish on its side; make 4-5 cuts on each side. Each cut should be at a 45° angle running toward the head of the fish. In each cut place a thin sliver of *fresh ginger.* Season with *salt* and *fresh ground black pepper;* dust with *corn starch.*

| In large pot for frying (with high temperature thermometer), heat... | 1 | gallon | *peanut oil* |

Heat oil to temperature
of between 350°-375°F.

Carefully place fish in hot oil for 8-10 minutes. Fish should be crispy on the outside, yet moist on the inside. Serve with Citrus Dipping Sauce; garnish with *watercress.*

Citrus Dipping Sauce

In bowl, combine...	2	tablespoons	*fresh orange juice*
	1	tablespoon	*fresh lemon juice*
	1	tablespoon	*rice wine vinegar*
	1	tablespoon	*soy sauce*

Mix well. Makes enough for one fish. Can be multiplied for additional servings.

"On occasion, I will recommend a beer. This is one of those times. The catfish offers a neutral, textural combination. The skin is crispy and the meat is somewhat firm. Try a light beer like an ale or a pilsner. These will be complementary. If you can find an Asian beer like Chung-hua or Yebisu, even better."

K.L.F., Master Sommelier

GRILLED BEEF STRIPLOIN
with CHILI-SCALLION SAUCE
Serves 4

For this recipe, you will need...	4	6 ounce	*beef striploins,* trimmed of excess fat
			salt
			black pepper, freshly ground
			peanut oil

Season striploins on both sides with *salt, fresh ground black pepper*. Brush with *peanut oil* and grill until done (3-4 minutes on each side for medium rare). To serve, slice striploins and spoon Chili-Scallion Sauce over top.

Chili-Scallion Sauce

In saucepan, over medium heat, add...	1	tablespoon	*peanut oil*
	1	teaspoon	*garlic,* minced
	1	teaspoon	*ginger,* minced
	1/4	teaspoon	*red chili flakes*

Cook until tender.

Add...	1/2	cup	*mirin* (sweet sake)
	1/4	cup	*soy sauce*
	1	tablespoon	*sugar*
Bring to a boil.			

In small cup, combine...	2	tablespoons	*cornstarch*
	1	tablespoon	*water*
Whisk into mirin mixture.			

Simmer for at least 5 minutes to incorporate starch and to thicken sauce.   Keep warm.

Just before serving, add...	1/4	cup	*scallions,* sliced

"There are two very important elements in this dish. First, the striploin is grilled. Grilling add intense flavors, sometimes smoky. Secondly, the sauce is sweet, viscous and has hints of spice. Overall, the dish is powerful and has weight. Try to find a red wine to accompany the dish and not to overwhelm it. My recommendation would be an Australian Grenache, plenty of fruit and a hint of acid to balance the sweet soy. Second choice might be a Spanish Tempranillo done in American oak."

K.L.F., Master Sommelier

The Merry Piglets
Mexican Grill

Merry Piglets has been satisfying Jackson Hole's desire for Mexican food since 1969, and enjoys a loyal following of locals and returning visitors. Opening as a small lunch/dinner 'stand' with large deck, 11 years ago Merry Piglets grew into a full-fledged restaurant. With a greatly expanded menu, it is not a mystery why 'Piglets' is so successful. They still make everything from scratch, from their creative and traditional dishes with homemade sauces and salsas, to cooking their own refried beans.

TORTILLA SOUP
Makes 2 Gallons

In large stockpot, combine...	5	pounds	*chicken thigh meat*
	2	gallons	*water*

Boil until chicken is thoroughly cooked. Strain chicken and reserve broth to add to soup. Chop chicken by hand into medium pieces.

In medium saucepan, combine...	1/2	cup	*garlic oil**
	4	cups	*white onions,* chopped
	1	bunch	*celery,* chopped
	1 1/2	tablespoons	*salt*
	1 1/2	tablespoons	*pepper*
Cook until vegetables are tender.			

Add...			*reserved broth*
			cooked chicken
	3	cups	*salsa*
Bring to boil. Reduce to simmer for half hour.			

To complete recipe, you will need...

tortilla strips, crisp
jack cheese, shredded
fresh cilantro,
coarsely chopped

To serve, ladle soup into bowls and sprinkle top with *crisp tortilla strips, jack cheese* and *chopped cilantro.*

BAJA ROLL with JALAPENO CREAM
and FRESH SALSA VERDE
Two Servings

For this recipe, you will need...			
	2	large	*flour tortilla*
	1/4	cup	*guacamole*
	1	small	*tomato,* diced
	2	handfuls	*fresh spinach,* chopped
	1	whole	*chicken breast,* cooked, diced
		OR	
	14	medium	*shrimp,* cooked

Lay a flour tortilla out flat. Lightly spread with **Jalapeno Cream Cheese**. Top with a light spread of *guacamole*, followed by a sprinkle of *diced tomatoes*. Follow that with *diced chicken breast* or *shrimp*, and place a large handful of *fresh spinach* on top. After placing all ingredients inside tortilla, roll the tortilla up and cut it down the middle. Secure with toothpicks. Serve fresh **Salsa Verde** on the side.

Jalapeno Cream Cheese

In mixing bowl, combine and
    mix well...

3/4	pound	*cream cheese*
1	tablespoon	*jalapenos,* diced

Using canned jalapenos will keep the temperature on the milder side. If you want it hot, increase amount or use fresh jalapenos! Store in covered container in refrigerator.

Salsa Verde

In blender or food processor, combine
    until well blended...

6-7	whole	*tomatillas,* canned
2	large	*garlic cloves,* crushed
1	cup	*sour cream*
1/2	cup	*mayonnaise*
1	bunch	*fresh cilantro*
1	cup	*jalapenos,* diced

Store in covered container in refrigerator.

Signal Mountain Lodge sits on the shores of Jackson Lake at the base of the Grand Tetons. What a view! I had dinner in their dining room, The Peaks Restaurant, just this summer. The Chicken Marsala was different from any I've ever had....and absolutely delicious! My friend had the Fresh Trout with Sundried Tomato-Raspberry Vinaigrette, and it was great also. I asked the chef that night if he would share the recipes in my book. He and his partner chef, Todd Baron, and Signal Mountain Lodge were happy to do so!

CHICKEN MARSALA
by Dan Hardy

Serves 4

In preparing this dish, be sure to allow time for the chicken breasts to marinate for an hour or two. Make the sauce ahead and, while the chicken finishs cooking in the oven, make the pasta.

For this recipe, you will need...	4	whole	**chicken breasts,** skinless, boneless, trimmed
	4-6	cups	**linguine,** cooked al dente

In bowl, combine...	1/4	cup	**olive oil**
	2	tablespoons	**white wine**
	2	tablespoons	**marsala**
	1	teaspoon	**garlic,** minced
	1/2	teaspoon	**thyme**
			salt and pepper

Place chicken breasts in marinade for 2 hours.

In skillet, over medium heat, sauté...		**chicken breasts**

Cook for 2 minutes on each side.
Remove to **preheated** 375° oven to finish.

In saucepan, over medium heat, combine...

3	tablespoons	*butter*
1	cup	*button mushrooms,* quartered
2	tablespoons	*garlic,* minced
1	tablespoon	*shallots,* minced
1	sprig	*thyme*
1	whole	*bay leaf*

Sauté for 5 minutes.

Add and simmer over low heat for 5 minutes...

3	tablespoons	*flour*

Add...

1 1/2	cups	*marsala wine*
1	cup	*chicken broth*
1/2	cup	*beef broth*

Simmer on lowest heat for 20 minutes. Add...

salt and pepper to taste

Serve chicken breasts with sauce, alongside Pasta.

Pasta

For this recipe, you will need...

4-6	cups	*linguine,* cooked al dente

In large sauté pan, combine...

1/4	cup	*olive oil*
1/2	cup	*button mushrooms,* quartered
2	tablespoons	*garlic,* minced
2	tablespoons	*shallots,* minced

Cook until shallots are translucent.

Add...	1	teaspoon	*fresh thyme,* chopped
	1	teaspoon	*fresh basil,* chopped
	1	teaspoon	*fresh sage,* chopped
	4	ounces	*white wine*
	4	ounces	*balsamic vinegar*

Reduce by half.

Add...	1/2	cup	*roma tomatoes,* diced
			salt and pepper to taste

Simmer another minute.

Swirl in...	3	tablespoons	*butter,* broken up

Add pasta and toss together.

FRESH TROUT with
SUNDRIED TOMATO-RASPBERRY VINAIGRETTE   Serves 4
by Todd Baron

This recipe is wonderfully simple and oh so delicious on fresh grilled trout! You can also make this a thinner consistency to use on salads by decreasing the amount of tomato and increasing the water.

For this recipe, you will need...	1 1/2	pounds	*fresh trout*

Grill or sauté trout just until done. Don't over cook! Top with Sundried Tomato- Raspberry Vinaigrette.

Sundried Tomato-Raspberry Vinaigrette

In blender or food processor, combine...	1	cup	*sundried tomatoes**
	2	cups	*hot water*
	1	ounce	*raspberry vinegar*
	1	tablespoon	*shallots*

	1	teaspoon	*garlic,* crushed
	1	teaspoon	*fresh thyme,* leaves only
	1	teaspoon	*fresh basil,* chopped *salt and pepper to taste*

| With machine running, slowly drizzle in... | 3 | ounces | *olive oil* |

Rehydrate tomatoes in hot water before using. When using sundried tomatoes packed in oil, drain them well before slicing.

GARLIC SOUP

Because of its popularity, this soup has been on the dinner menu at the Peaks Restaurant Lodge for several years.

In large baking pan, toss together...	1/2	pound	*garlic cloves,* peeled
	1	cup	*olive oil*
Roast in **preheated** 275° oven for 45-60 minutes. Drain off oil.			

In large saucepan, combine...			*roasted garlic*
	3	ounces	*butter*
	1/4	cup	*red onion,* sliced
	1/4	cup	*white onion,* sliced
Sauté until onions are translucent.			

| Add... | 1/2 | cup | *flour* |
| Stir and cook 2-3 minutes. | | | |

| Add... | 1/4 | cup | *sherry* |
| Reduce by half. | | | |

Add...	4	cups	*beef broth**
	2	teaspoons	*thyme*
	2	teaspoons	*sage*
	1	whole	*bay leaf*
Simmer 1 hour.			

| Remove bay leaf; add... | 3/4 | cup | *heavy cream* |
| | 1 | tablespoon | *basil* |

Puree in food processor until smooth. Season to taste with *salt and pepper.*

Rising Sage is a wonderful cafe located in the National Museum of Wildlife Art across from the National Elk Refuge, about 3 miles north of the town of Jackson. After strolling through 14 galleries viewing the most beautiful wildlife paintings and sculpture, it is especially nice to enjoy a snack or lunch while gazing out the windows (or from the terrace) at the glorious, panoramic view of the Elk Refuge, the Gros Ventre mountain range and the Yellowstone range to the north!

ROASTED TOMATO SOUP
by Chef Tom Henninger   Serves 12-16

On greased baking sheet, place...	12	ripe	*tomatoes,* quartered
Combine...	2	tablespoons	*olive oil*
	1	large clove	*garlic,* minced

Brush tomatoes with garlic and oil. Roast in **preheated** 350° oven until golden brown for approximately 30 minutes.

In stock pot, combine...	$^{1}/_{2}$	cup	*butter*
	1	large clove	*garlic,* minced
	2	large	*onions,* chopped
Sauté until onions are tender.			

Add...	1	quart	*tomato sauce*
Bring to a slow boil. Add...	2	quarts	*chicken broth*
			roasted tomatoes
Cook for 2 minutes, then puree in food processor.			

Return soup to stockpot. Add...	2	quarts	*heavy cream*
	1	cup	*parmesan cheese*
			shredded
	1	bunch	*fresh basil,* chopped
			salt and pepper
			to taste

Bring soup to a low simmer to meld and thicken. If the soup is too thin for your preference (or if you would like to cut back on the amount of heavy cream), you can thicken it with *roux*. Make roux in small pan by melting $1/4$ cup butter and stirring in $1/4$ cup flour. Allow to cook, while stirring, for 1 minute. Add to soup a little at a time, stirring constantly, until you have the desired consistency.

CHIPOLTE MAYONNAISE

by Chef Tom Henninger   Makes 2 cups

This is great by itself as a vegetable dip, as a sandwich spread or on salads.

In bowl, combine...	2	cups	*mayonnaise*
	1	small can	*chipolte peppers,*
			finely diced
	1	teaspoon	*fresh lemon juice*
	1	teaspoon	*black pepper*
	1	teaspoon	*cumin*
	1	teaspoon	*salt*

CURRY CHICKEN SALAD
by Chef John Jefferson

This is delicous as an appetizer with croutons, as a sandwich on good bread, or with fresh greens in a salad. Please note, when using as an appetizer, mince or finely chop all ingredients. When used in a sandwich or salad, coarsely **chop** *ingredients.*

In mixing bowl, combine...	5	8 ounce	*chicken breasts** cooked, chopped
	$^2/_3$	cup	*mayonnaise*
	$^2/_3$	cup	*pistachios,* chopped
	$^1/_2$	cup	*dried apricots,* chopped
	$^1/_3$	cup	*green onions,* chopped
	$^1/_3$	cup	*honey*
	2	tablespoons	*fresh thyme,* leaves only, chopped
	2	tablespoons	*curry powder*
	1	tablespoon	*garlic,* minced *salt and pepper to taste*

| In sandwich, salad or appetizer, garnish with... | *fresh cilantro leaf* |

*For moist, tender chicken, a great way to cook it is to place boneless chicken breasts in baking pan; cover with milk. Bake, uncovered, in preheated 350° oven for about 35 minutes, until done. Drain off milk. Let chicken cool. Refrigerate until ready to use.

Stagecoach Grill

The Stagecoach Grill, a new cafe owned by Dave Iantuono and Scott Interdonato, serves up a terrific lunch and dinner at the Stagecoach Bar, in Wilson. Since the 1930s, the Stagecoach has been the place to be when looking for fun! Most especially on Sunday afternoon and evenings, the merriment hits a fevered pitch. For 31 years, Bill Briggs and his Stagecoach Band have created the greatest revelry on Sundays, playing western swing music. Visitors who have found their way to the 'Coach' on a Sunday, go home with a story to tell!

CHICKEN QUESADILLA with FRESH SALSA

For this recipe, you will need...

1	whole	*boneless chicken breast*
		cumin
		salt and pepper
2	10"	*flour tortillas*
		sour cream

Season *chicken breast* with *cumin*, *salt* and *pepper*. Slice.

On flat cook top or griddle, over medium heat, sear one side of one *tortilla*.

Turn over and sprinkle
seared side with...

3	ounces	*cheddar cheese,* shredded
3	ounces	*jack cheese,* shredded
1	tablespoon	*fresh cilantro,* chopped
1	tablespoon	*red onion,* thinly sliced
2	ounces	*tomato,* diced
		sliced chicken

Place the other tortilla on top. Cook until bottom tortilla is slightly crisped, flip over. Cook until tortilla on bottom is slightly crisped and cheese has melted. Serve with sour cream and Salsa.

Salsa

In bowl, combine and mix well...

15	whole	*tomatoes,* diced
1	whole	*red onion* diced
1/2	bunch	*fresh cilantro,* chopped
5	whole	*fresh jalapenos,* diced
3	cloves	*garlic,* minced
4	whole	*limes,* juice of
1	teaspoon	*cumin*

PART III

Great Cooks I Know....
And a Few Recipes of My Own!

It's been ten years since I sold my restaurant, Cafe Christine. But even now, people occasionally reminisce about the Cafe and tell me they wish it was still there. To all of you with fond memories....thank you!

Over the years, I've had many requests for recipes. There are several which are asked for frequently. I thought it would be a good idea to include, as part of my recipe contribution, some of those recipes.

One recipe in particular has been asked for more than any other....the Oriental Salad Dressing. I've never shared it, because for a number of years, I was bottling and selling it to local grocers. That endeavor behind me, it's a good time to share it! The foundation of the recipe was the brainchild of my sister-in-law, Deborah, from which I developed the recipe used at Cafe Christine.

ORIENTAL SALAD DRESSING

Makes 1 Quart

This will keep for weeks in your refrigerator. It is super on any green salad, and is dynamite on spinach salads with egg, crumbled bacon and mushrooms, or even on salads with fruit.

In food processor or blender combine...	$1/4$	cup	*honey*
	$1/4$	cup	*soy sauce*
	1	tablespoon	*fresh garlic,* minced
Process until well blended.			

Add...	$1/2$	cup	*red wine vinegar*
	$1^1/4$	tablespoons	*fresh lemon juice*
Blend thoroughly.			

| With machine running, slowly add... | $1^1/2$ | cups | *vegetable oil* |
| Blend to fully emulsify. | | | |

| Add and blend well... | 1 | | *egg white* |
| (this is optional) | | | |

The dressing is just fine without the egg white. We found that adding some egg white gave the dressing more body, therefore it would cling nicely to the lettuce; something that was better for presentation in a restaurant, but not necessary at home.

Other flavor options you may
wish to try...

Replace $1/2$ cup canola oil with...	$1/2$	cup	*sesame oil*
And/or, add...	1	teaspoon	*fresh ginger,* grated

POPPY SEED SALAD DRESSING Makes 1 Quart

Another favorite salad dressing of Cafe Christine's guests.

In food processor or blender combine...	1	cup	*vegetable oil*
	$1/2$	cup	*brown sugar*
	$1/2$	cup	*red onion,* chopped
Process thoroughly.			

Add...	$2/3$	cup	*red wine vinegar*
	2	teaspoons	*dijon mustard*
	$1^1/2$	teaspoons	*salt*
	$1/2$	teaspoon	*black pepper*
	$1^1/2$	tablespoons	*poppy seeds*

With machine running, slowly add...	1	cup	*vegetable oil*
Blend to emulsify.			

CAJUN SPICE

For my taste, most cajun spices available in the marketplace have too much salt in them. So, we made our own at Cafe Christine. This cajun spice was so popular that I packaged and sold it. Another recipe that I haven't shared up until now. Don't be hesitant to experiment. Make your own, emphasizing herbs you really like.

Mix together...

2	tablespoons	*paprika*
1	tablespoon	*cayenne*
1	tablespoon	*garlic powder*
1	tablespoon	*onion powder*
$2^1/_2$	teaspoons	*thyme*
$2^1/_2$	teaspoons	*marjorum*
$1^1/_2$	teaspoons	*oregano*
$1^1/_2$	teaspoons	*cumin*
$1^1/_2$	teaspoons	*white pepper*
$1^1/_2$	teaspoons	*black pepper*
$1^1/_2$	teaspoons	*salt*

CAESAR SALAD

Serves 6

Cafe Christine was well known for its caesar salad. This recipe is in my first book, but because of its popularity, I thought it should be included once again! Anyone who likes their caesar salad with a strong flavor or bite, with a noticeable flavor of garlic, will love this! If you are a fan of milder caesar salads, you will want to use the dressing recipe from Jenny Lake Lodge, a wonderful, milder version.

Caesar salad, especially with a freshly grilled or sautéed chicken breast on top, is a great meal all by itself. It's my daughter's favorite dinner!

For this recipe, you will need...

1-2	heads	*romaine*

Wash, drain well and tear into bite-size pieces. (One large handful per serving.)

1-2	cups	*croutons* (homemade, see recipe on p.207)
$1/_2$-1	cup	*parmesan cheese,* freshly grated or shredded

It is very important when making a caesar salad that the romaine is <u>cold</u> and <u>crisp</u> before tossing with the dressing and parmesan cheese. Place prepared romaine into a cloth bag (a pillow case works well) and chill in refrigerator 2 hours before serving.

Just before serving, toss romaine with desired amounts of *caesar dressing, parmesan cheese,* and *croutons.* Start with about 1 cup of dressing, you can always add more if you like a 'wetter' salad.

Caesar salad preferences range far and wide....light or heavy with the dressing....grated or shredded parmesan cheese,...lots of croutons or not too many. Find what you like and do it!

Caesar Dressing (Makes 1 Quart)

Be sure to make the dressing several hours ahead so it will have time to chill in the refrigerator.

In food processor or blender, puree until smooth...	1	2 oz. can	*anchovies,* drained
	8	teaspoons	*fresh garlic,* smashed
	1/4	cup	*olive oil*
Add and process until well mixed...	2/3	cup	*red wine vinegar**
	2 1/2	tablespoons	*dijon mustard*
	2	teaspoons	*worcestershire sauce*
	1/2	teaspoon	*salt*
	1/2	teaspoon	*black pepper*
	1/2	cup	*lemon,* juice of
With machine running, slowly add...	1 3/4	cups	*olive oil*
Followed by...	3	large	*eggs,* one at a time

Continue blending for 4-5 seconds after adding the last egg to completely emulsify. Chill in refrigerator. Dressing is at its best for about 3 days.

Sometimes I use half red wine vinegar and half balsamic vinegar.

Croutons*

Cut into cubes...	**1**	loaf	*french bread*
Sprinkle lightly with...			*salt*
			white pepper
			garlic powder
			basil, dried
			marjoram, diced
Drizzle evenly with...			*melted butter*
			(or) olive oil

Bake in **preheated** 400° oven for 10-15 minutes, until dry and light golden brown. If you want to take the time, browning croutons in a hot skillet [while stirring or shaking pan often] before baking makes them even more delicious! It's easy enough to do if you make a small batch.

This recipe makes more than you will need for this salad, but they keep almost indefinitely when stored in a sealed bag or container in the freezer. They also make great bread crumbs for other recipes....just crush them up in a processor or blender.

BEEF STROGANOFF

We changed our menu with each new season, year to year. This is the one dish that, except for one season, remained on the menu for the entire six years. I had so many requests for it, we brought it back and always kept it on the menu.

A great beef stroganoff is the result of two equally important factors: making a rich, delicious sauce and using beef tenderlion filet! The mistake many people make is they use an inexpensive cut of beef. Splurge....use only the best cut of beef for this dish!

This is a great entree for entertaining, or for those nights when you know you won't want to spend a lot of time in the kitchen. You can make the sauce a day or two ahead, and even slice up your vegetables and meat; and then later, throw it all together in a matter of minutes.

In a large skillet, over medium high heat, melt...	3	tablespoons	*butter*
Add...	1	pound	*mushrooms,** sliced
	2	medium	*yellow onions,* julienned

Sauté until mushrooms and onions are tender and slightly golden. Remove from pan; set aside.

In same skillet, over high heat, add...	2	pounds	*beef tenderloin* thinly sliced on the diagonal

Sauté the pieces of filet quickly on both sides. DON'T overcook them. You may need to cook the meat in two batches. If so, transfer the cooked pieces to a plate while you cook the next batch.

When all the meat is sautéed, add the sautéed mushrooms and onions back into the skillet, and stir in about 2 cups of the **Stroganoff Sauce**. How much sauce you add will depend on how 'saucy' you like it. Bring to a simmer and cook for about 2 minutes. Serve over pasta of choice or rice. It's great both ways.

Great Variation

When adding the sautéed mushrooms and onions back into the skillet, also add $^1/_2$ cup freshly diced roma tomatoes (seeded), and $^1/_4$ cup sliced green onions. Cook for half a minute before adding sauce.

We called this Stroganoff Vermeer, named after one of my chefs who always made this for his own dinner. It was so good, we served our stroganoff this way the last two years. Chad Vermeer is now the chef at Snake River Brewery.

At Cafe Christine we used white mushrooms. Now, I use shitake or portabella mushrooms. It is even more delicious!

Stroganoff Sauce

In heavy sauce pan, combine...

1	cup	*heavy cream*
2	cups	*sour cream*
3	tablespoons	*tomato paste*
3	tablespoons	*Worcestershire*
4	teaspoons	*dijon mustard*
$2^1/_2$	teaspoons	*paprika*
2	teaspoons	*beef base*

Simmer over low heat for 20 minutes, stirring occasionally.

Remove from heat and stir in...   2   **tablespoons**   *dry sherry*

If you choose to make the sauce ahead, allow it to cool completely before covering and storing in refrigerator. After refrigeration, it will be quite thick. You don't need to thin or reheat it before adding it to the meat. Just spoon as much of the sauce as you want into the pan with the cooked meat, onions and mushrooms and simmer for about 2 minutes.

And now for desserts!

I love to bake as much as I love to cook. In fact, I believe I love baking even more than cooking. Baking is very soothing and fulfilling for me. When I am stressed or facing a difficult task, I will often escape to the kitchen to bake. It's probably my best form of procrastination!

Many of the desserts we featured at Cafe Christine were not particularly fancy, just really good! Of all the tasks it takes to run a restaurant successfully, baking desserts and breads was pure pleasure for me. I really enjoy experimenting and creating new recipes. Desserts were freshly made, and different every night at the Cafe.

Two of my favorite desserts are cheesecakes and bread puddings. There are a hundred different ways to make both. Here are just a few...

BASIC CHEESECAKE

To keep it simple, here is the basic recipe, from which to begin the filling and crust of all the cheese-cakes. Following this basic recipe are the variations.

In mixing bowl, combine...	$1^1/_2$	pounds	*cream cheese*
	$^3/_4$	cup	*sugar*
Beat well, occasionally scraping bowl, until smooth.			

Add...	5	large	*eggs,* one at a time
Mix thoroughly after each egg is added. Scrap bowl often.			

Add...			*flavorings* (different for each cheesecake; see separate recipes)
Mix thoroughly.			

Pour mixture into baked **Cookie Crust**. Bake in a water bath (with water halfway up the springform pan) in a **preheated** 375° oven for $1^1/_4$ to $1^1/_2$ hours. It will rise quite high. The cheesecake is done when the center is firm to the touch, and afterwards, springs back.

Carefully remove cheesecake from water bath and remove from oven. Immediately and gently take the foil off the pan and set cheesecake on a rack to cool completely. As it is cooling, the cheesecake will drop. [If the sides of your cookie crust are high up on the pan, they will curl or wrap over the top edge of the cheesecake, which makes for a very nice presentation.] If the cookie crust sides are not high, that's okay too. It still looks good!

Leave cheesecake in the springform pan, cover with plastic and refrigerate until serving. Remove from refrigerator 20-30 minutes before serving. It will be more flavorful if it is not so cold when eaten.

Chocolate Cookie Crust

In food processor, combine...	3	ounces	*Famous Chocolate Wafer Cookies*
	3	ounces	*chocolate graham crackers*
	3	ounces	*vanilla wafers*
Process until finely crushed.			

With machine running, add...	$^1/_4$	cup	*butter,* melted
	2	tablespoons	*Kahlua*

Mix until thoroughly blended. Spread the crumbs evenly into a 9" springform cake pan, and press firmly to create a $^1/_4$" thick crust. Make sure to press the crumbs up the side as far as possible, to within an inch of the top of the pan. Take care to create a nice angle where the side and bottom of the pan meet. Bake in **preheated** 350° oven for 10-11 minutes. Allow to cool completely.

IMPORTANT: To avoid getting any water into the crust while baking in a water bath, place the pan in the center of a large piece of foil; large enough to wrap the foil up the sides to the very top. Fold over any excess and press the foil firmly in place.

Vanilla Cookie Crust

In food processor, combine...	$4^1/_2$	ounces	*vanilla wafers*
	$4^1/_2$	ounces	*graham crackers*
Process until finely crushed.			

With machine running, add...	$^1/_4$	cup	*butter,* melted
	2	tablespoons	*Amaretto*

To complete, follow method described in the **Chocolate Cookie Crust** recipe above.

MOCHA CHOCOLATE CHIP CHEESECAKE

We often featured cheesecake at Cafe Christine. This is still my favorite.

Using the *Basic Recipe* on previous page, when you have thoroughly blended the eggs into the cream cheese mixture...

Add...	2	tablespoons	*Kahlua*
	1¹/₂	tablespoons	*espresso*
	¹/₄	cup	*semi-sweet chocolate shavings*

Mix thoroughly.

Pour into baked **Chocolate Cookie Crust**, and follow instructions of *Basic Recipe* .

RASPBERRY AMARETTO CHEESECAKE

*When fresh raspberries are readily available, be sure to try this cheesecake! This cheesecake is delicious in either the **Chocolate Cookie Crust** or the **Vanilla Cookie Crust.** It just depends on what you are in the mood for!*

For this recipe, you will need.   1   cup   *fresh raspberries*

Using the *Basic Recipe* on previous page, when you have thoroughly blended the eggs into the cream cheese mixture...

Add...	2	tablespoons	*Amaretto*
	1	teaspoon	*almond extract*
	1	teaspoon	*vanilla extract*

Mix thoroughly.

Pour into baked cookie crust of choice. Gently drop the *fresh raspberies,* one by one onto the top of the cheesecake. They should sink in a bit, but the topes of the raspberries will still show. To complete preparation, follow baking instructions of *Basic Recipe* .

PUMPKIN CHEESECAKE

Using the *Basic Recipe* on previous page, when you have thoroughly blended the eggs into the cream cheese mixture...

Add...			
	1	pound	*pumpkin,* canned
	2	tablespoons	*Frangelico*
	1	teaspoon	*vanilla extract*
	1	teaspoon	*cinnamon*
	$1/4$	teaspoon	*ginger*
	$1/4$	teaspoon	*nutmeg*
	$1/4$	teaspoon	*cloves*

Mix thoroughly.

Pour into baked **Pecan Cookie Crust**, and follow instructions of *Basic Recipe* .

Pecan Cookie Crust

In food processor, combine...			
	$4^1/2$	ounces	*vanilla wafers*
	$4^1/2$	ounces	*graham crackers*
	$1/4$	cup	*pecans,* chopped

Process until finely crushed.

With machine running, add...			
	$1/4$	cup	*butter,* melted
	2	tablespoons	*Frangelico*

To complete, follow the procedure for the **Chocolate Cookie Crust** on previous page.

PEANUT BUTTER CHOCOLATE CHEESECAKE

*Anyone who loves Reeses Peanut Butter will **love** this!*

In mixing bowl, combine...	$1^1/_2$	pounds	*cream cheese*
	$1^1/_2$	cups	*creamy peanut butter*
	$^1/_2$	cup	*sugar*
	$^1/_2$	cup	*brown sugar*
Beat well, occasionally scraping bowl, until smooth with no lumps.			

Add...	5	large	*eggs,* one at a time
Mix thoroughly after each egg is added. Scrap bowl often.			

Add...	1	tablespoon	*heavy cream*
	3	teaspoons	*macadamia nut liqueur*
	2	teaspoons	*vanilla extract*
Mix thoroughly.			

Pour into baked **Chocolate Cookie Crust**, and follow instructions of basic recipe on the previous page, up to the point the cheesecake has finished baking. Carefully remove cheesecake from water bath and remove from oven. Immediately pour **Chocolate Cream** over the top, making sure it spreads all the way to the edges. Put the cheesecake back in the oven (without water bath) for 6 minutes. Remove from oven and allow to cool, as described in basic recipe.

Chocolate Cream

In small saucepan, combine...	$^1/_4$	cup	*butter*
	2	tablespoons	*water*
	2	tablespoons	*corn syrup*
Cook over medium heat until it just comes to a boil. Remove from heat.			

Stir in...	4	ounces	*semi-sweet chocolate chips*
Whisk until smooth and shiny. Allow *chocolate sauce* to cool slightly.			

In small bowl, mix well...	$^3/_4$	cup	*sour cream*
	1	large	*egg yolk*
	2	tablespoons	*sugar*

| Whisk in, until thoroughly blended... | $^1/_2$ | cup | *chocolate sauce* |

Taste the sauce. If you want it to have a stronger chocolate taste, you can add another 2 to 4 tablespoons chocolate sauce.

BANANA ALMOND PRALINE CHEESECAKE

Using the *Basic Recipe* on page *210*, when you have thoroughly blended the eggs into the cream cheese mixture...

Add...	2	tablespoons	*Banana Liqueur*
	1	teaspoon	*vanilla extract*
Mix thoroughly.			

| Place on botton of crust, a layer of... | | | *banana slices* |
| | | | ($^1/_4$ " slices) |

Pour the cheesecake batter over the banana slices on the bottom of the baked **Almond Cookie Crust**. Follow instructions of *Basic Recipe*, up to the point the cheesecake has finished baking. Carefully remove cheesecake from water bath and remove from oven. Immediately pour **Sour Cream Mixture** over the top, making sure it spreads all the way to the edges. Sprinkle top with **Candied Almonds**; put the cheesecake back in the oven (without water bath) for 6 minutes. Remove from oven and allow to cool, as described in *Basic Recipe*.

Almond Cookie Crust

In food processor, combine...	$4^1/_2$	ounces	*vanilla wafers*
	$4^1/_2$	ounces	*graham crackers*
	$^1/_4$	cup	*pecans,* chopped

Process cookies and nuts
until finely crushed.

| With machine running, add... | ¹/₄ | cup | *butter,* melted |
| | 2 | tablespoons | *Frangelico* |

To complete, follow the procedure for the **Chocolate Cookie Crust** on page *211*.

Sour Cream/Almond Topping

In mixing bowl, combine and mix well...	1	cup	*sour cream*
	1	large	*egg yolk*
	2	tablespoons	*sugar*

Candied Almonds

In small saucepan, combine...	2	tablespoons	*butter*
	2¹/₂	tablespoons	*brown sugar*
	¹/₃	cup	*almonds,* chopped
	¹/₄	teaspoon	*cinnamon*

Cook over medium heat, stirring constantly, for 2 minutes. Remove from heat and spread nuts on a plate. Allow to cool completely. Break into small pebble-like pieces.

PEAR BRANDY BREAD PUDDING

I made lots of different bread puddings at the Cafe. The favorite seemed to be this one. Many recipes call for a lot more butter and heavy cream. Using less butter and half and half still makes a rich bread pudding. You just don't have to worry near as much about having a heart attack!

For this recipe, you will need...	1	loaf	*french bread,* two days old, torn into small pieces
	3	large	*bartlett pears,* peeled, cored, sliced
		OR	
	2	15 oz. cans	*pears,* well drained

In mixing bowl, combine...	$^1/_2$	cup	*butter,* room temperature
	2	cups	*sugar*
Beat for about 5 minutes, until thoroughly creamed and fluffy, scraping bowl occasionally.			

Add, two at a time, mixing well between each addition...	10	large	*eggs*

With mixer turned to low, slowly add...	1	quart	*half and half*
	$^1/_4$	cup	*pear brandy*

Spread *sliced pears* evenly in the bottom of an oiled 9" x 15" baking pan. Cover pears and fill baking pan to within 1" of top with torn pieces of bread. Pour custard mixture over the top, completely drenching all the bread. Allow to sit for 30 minutes. Bake in water bath (with water halfway up the side of pan) in a **preheated** 350° oven for one hour, until slightly golden and custard has set. Remove from oven. Allow to cool for 20-30 minutes before serving. Serve with dollop of real whipped cream (no whipped *toppings!*)

CHOCOLATE KAHLUA BREAD PUDDING

Use the same preparation as the Pear Brandy Bread Pudding, with these exceptions...

•   Use two-day old chocolate cake instead of french bread.

•   When making custard, substitute Kahlua for the pear brandy; substitute 1 cup of sugar with brown sugar; add $^1/_2$ teaspoon of cinnamon.

•   Drizzle each serving with warm **Chocolate Glaze**.

Chocolate Glaze

In small saucepan, combine...	$^1/_2$	cup	*butter*
	$^1/_2$	cup	*corn syrup*
	$^1/_3$	cup	*water*
Cook, over medium heat, until it just comes to a boil.			

| Remove from heat and stir in... | 8 | ounces | *semi-sweet chocolate chips* |
| | 3 | tablespoons | *Kahlua* |

Whisk until smooth and shiny. Serve warm.

JAMAICAN RUM COCONUT BREAD PUDDING

Use the same preparation as the Pear Brandy Bread Pudding, with these exceptions...

•   Use two-day old white cake instead of french bread. Toss broken up cake pieces with one cup fresh pineapple (diced, small).

•   When making custard, substitute dark rum for the pear brandy.

•   Before pouring custard mixture over broken up cake pieces, sprinkle with $1/4$ to $1/3$ cup toasted coconut.   [Toast in skillet over medium heat. Shake and toss coconut until lightly golden.]

•   Serve with warm Sauce Anglaise.

Sauce Anglaise

| In saucepan, combine... | 2 | cups | *milk* |
| | 1 | whole | *vanilla bean* |

Bring to a scald. Remove from heat. Remove vanilla bean.

In mixing bowl, combine...	1	cup	*sugar*
	8	large	*egg yolks*
	1	pinch	*salt*

Whisk together until it is shiny and ribbon-like.

Transfer sugar-egg mixture to heavy saucepan. While whisking, slowly add... **warm milk** (not hot)

With saucepan over medium heat, stir continuously until the first signs of boiling and custard clings to the back of a spoon. Remove from heat and strain through fine sieve. Serve warm or cold.

Well known throughout the country and in many parts of the world for her wonderfully creative, flamboyant, colorful art, Audrey celebrates her birthday each Halloween by putting up a batch of Pickled Pumpkin. I am a huge fan of Audrey's, and so happy to share her recipe. A great condiment with turkey/meats, it is also a super in stir-frys.

"Part of a peck of PICKLED PUMPKIN"

For this recipe, you will need...	1	large	*pumpkin*

Cut pumpkin into sections; pare skin off; clean out seeds and 'hair'. After cleaning each section, cut into cubes. Immerse in pickling **marinade** overnight.

The following day, bring pumpkin and **pickling marinade** to a boil. Reduce heat and simmer until pumpkin is semi-transparant, but <u>still firm</u>. Remove pumpkin and continue simmering marinade to thicken slightly. Return pumpkin to liquid and bring to boil once more. Place pumpkin into sterilized jars; fill jars nearly full with liquid and some of the pickling spices. Secure lids and allow to cool.

Pickling Marinade

In large pot, combine...	6	cups	*water*
	6	cups	*white vinegar*
	6	cups	*white sugar*
	2"	piece	*fresh ginger,* peeled, diced
	3	tablespoons	*pickling spice**
	1	small	*bay leaf*

Bring to a boil; reduce to simmer for 15 minutes. Taste for personal approval. Audrey likes it to have a sharp taste with a slight sweetness. You can adjust the sweetness or spiciness. When the marinade is the way you like it, allow it to cool some before adding pumpkin.

*If you can't get pickling spice; substitute with 8 cloves, 4 whole allspice, $1/2$ teaspoon mustard seed, and a small piece of cinnamon.

Bill Boney is a professional caterer who creates the most terrific fare. Whether catering small intimate dinner parties or parties for groups of 500 and more, he makes it look easy. His dishes are always so scrumptious and creative. Bill has given us a sampling of some of his hors d'oeuvres.

GRILLED SALMON SKEWERS
with LIME BBQ GLAZE

For this recipe, you will need...	1	pound	*fresh salmon filet*
			boned, skin off
	2	tablespoons	*white sesame seeds*
	2	tablespoons	*black sesame seeds*
	2	tablespoons	*fresh chives,* chopped

Slice on angle across the filet to create rectangular strips $1^1/_2$" long, $^3/_4$" wide, $^1/_4$" to $^1/_2$" thick. Thread onto bamboo skewers and dip into one portion of the Lime Glaze.

Grill to desired doneness and drizzle with some of the reserved Lime Glaze. Sprinkle with *sesame seeds* and *fresh chopped chives.* Serve.

Lime Glaze

In mixing bowl, combine...	1	bottle	*BBQ sauce of choice*
	$^1/_4$	cup	*lime juice,*
			fresh squeezed
	2	tablespoons	*roasted garlic,*
			crushed

Blend well and separate glaze into two containers; one for dipping uncooked salmon into before grilling, and one to drizzle over skewered salmon after its cooked.

SMOKED TROUT and GOAT CHEESE
on CRISP APPLE SLICES

For this recipe, you will need...	1/4 - 1/2	pound	*smoked trout,* skinless
	1-2	whole	*granny smith apples,* halved, seeded
	1-2	tablespoons	*parsley* (for garnish) finely chopped

Slice *apples* into thick slices; spoon or pipe Herbed Goat Cheese onto apple slice and top with bite size piece of *smoked trout.* Sprinkle with chopped parsley and serve.

Herbed Goat Cheese

In mixer, combine...	8	ounces	*goat cheese*
	1	tablespoon	*shallots,* finely minced
	3	tablespoons	*fresh basil,* minced
	3	tablespoons	*dried tomato,* *finely* diced

Vegetable amounts can be varied in accordance to taste.

HAZELNUT CHICKEN BITES
WRAPPED with PROSCIUTTO

For this recipe, you will need...	1	pound	*chicken breasts,* skinless, boneless
	1/2	pound	*prosciutto,* sliced paper thin
	1	cup	*hazelnuts,* toasted, finely ground
			flour, seasoned with salt and pepper
			egg wash
			toothpicks

Cut chicken into bite size pieces. Dredge pieces of chicken in *seasoned flour,* next in *egg wash* and finally in *finely ground hazelnuts.*

Sauté chicken in hot olive oil to brown on all sides. Remove from pan to paper towel lined sheet pan to cool. Wrap each chicken bite with paper thin slice of *prosciutto* and secure with a toothpick.

Place skewered chicken bites on sheet pan and flash bake in **preheated** 400° oven to reheat.

    Drizzle with...   ***lemon butter***

    Sprinkle with...   ***parmesan cheese***

Celebrating Christmas Eve, enjoying Dad's swedish meatballs with egg noodles and lingonberries, is a favorite tradition for the Burklands. Bruce makes the meatballs ahead, so there's plenty of time to enjoy their Christmas tree relaxing by the fire.

SWEDISH MEATBALLS

| In dutch oven, sauté until onions are translucent... | 1 | tablespoon | *butter,* melted |
| | 1 | cup | *onions,* chopped |

In mixing bowl, combine...			*sautéed onions*
	1	pound	*ground turkey*
	1	pound	*ground beef* (lean)
	3/4	cup	*bread crumbs*
	2	whole	*eggs,* beaten
	1/4	cup	*milk*
	1	teaspoon	*salt*
	3/4	teaspoon	*pepper*

Form mixture into meatballs. Makes about 2 dozen. Brown meatballs in same dutch oven in which onions were sautéed. Set meatballs aside.

| In pot of boiling salted water, add... | 1 | pound | *baby carrots* |

Cook until almost tender, 5-8 minutes. Rinse in cold water.

In same dutch oven, combine...	1/4	cup	*butter,* melted
	1/4	cup	*flour*
Stir and cook a few minutes. Stir in...	2	cups	*milk*
	1	cup	*chicken broth*

Bring to a simmer, whisking constantly. Simmer until thick.

| Whisk in... | 1 | cup | *half and half cream* |
| | 2 | tablespoons | *dijon mustard* |

Bring back to a simmer.

Add...

meatballs
cooked carrots
salt and pepper to
taste

Simmer until meatballs are
cooked through, 10-20 minutes.

Stir in...

fresh dill to taste

Serve immediately with...

egg noodles
lingonberries.

Can be made ahead of time. Cool, refrigerate before adding dill. After reheating meatballs and sauce, add fresh dill. Enjoy!

Bruce is one of the nicest persons I've ever known; and is a fantastic cook to boot! Though he spends his working hours pursuing other endeavors, he most enjoys spending time in the kitchen. He especially likes creating "bold flavored" recipes. Here are two prime examples!

HABANERO CREAM CHEESE MASHED POTATOES

"If any of your guests put gravy on these, they should be taken out in the backyard and summarily shot!!!"   Bruce Springer

For this recipe, you will need...	4	pounds	*russet potatoes,* peeled, halved
In food processor, or with a beater, combine...	1/2	cup	*butter,* room temperature
	8	ounces	*cream cheese,* room temperature
	1/2	cup	*milk*
	1	whole	*fresh habanero pepper,* seeds and ribs removed; finely minced

Process until smooth. Set aside to allow flavors to blend while potatoes cook. Do not refrigerate.

Boil potatoes until just done. Run them through a ricer. [If you do not have a ricer, use whatever method you normally use for mashing potatoes.] Put cream cheese mixture in the microwave for 30-60 seconds to warm it slightly so as not to cool down the potatoes when added.

Combine potatoes and cream cheese mixture until creamy. You may find that you need to add additional milk to achieve the proper consistency. If so, make sure the milk is hot. Place potatoes in serving dish and top with a slice of butter if desired and a sprinkle of paprika for color. Serve piping hot (a little blast in the microwave won't hurt just before serving).

JALAPENO APPLESAUCE

Serve hot or cold. This may be used as a condiment for baked ham or any kind of pork. Bruce uses granny smith apples, but mentioned that using your favorite cooking apple is fine. "A little of this sauce is really good on a ham sandwich!!" Bruce Springer

In large fry pan, combine...	2	tablespoons	*butter,* melted
	4		*granny smith apples,* cored, peeled, cut up
	1		*fresh jalapeno pepper,* chopped (seeds and all)
	$^1/_4$	cup	*brown sugar,* packed
	$^1/_2$	teaspoon	*cinnamon* (more if you like)

Sauté until the apples are fully cooked. Process the entire mixture in a food processor to a smooth consistency.

Jalapenos vary a lot in size and heat, so you may want to adjust the recipe to your taste before you make it the next time. If this is absolutely too hot for your taste, sauté a couple more apples and add to the mix.

She can't play a guitar, but she's a whiz in the kitchen! After owning two of her own coffee bistros, 'Ciao! Baby', in the Seattle area, Cat returned to Jackson Hole. Her baked delights are fabulous. Here is just a sampling.

BANANA CRUNCH MUFFINS

This recipe also makes a wonderful layer cake...delicious with a burnt butter frosting.

In large mixing bowl, combine...	3	cups	*flour*
	$1^1/_2$	cups	*sugar*
	$1^1/_2$	teaspoons	*baking powder*
	$3/_4$	teaspoon	*baking soda*
	$1/_2$	teaspoon	*cinnamon*
	$1/_2$	teaspoon	*salt*

In another bowl, combine...	$1^1/_2$	cups	*sour cream*
	3	large	*eggs*
	$1/_4$ cup + 2	tablespoons	*butter,* melted
	3	ripe	*bananas,* mashed ($1^1/_2$ cups)
Beat until well blended. Add...	$3/_4$	cup	*pecans* (optional)

Combine wet ingredients with dry, blend until just moistened. It will be lumpy. Pour into greased and floured, or lined, muffin pans; top with Streusel. Bake in **preheated** 375° oven for 20-25 minutes (toothpick inserted in center should come out clean).

If baking this recipe in a single layer cake or loaf pan, adjust heat for either of these as follows: cake pan (doubling this recipe makes three 8" rounds) at 350° for 20 minutes; 9x5 loaf pan (this recipe makes 1) at 325° for 35-40 minutes.

Streusel Topping

Combine...	2	cups	*flour*
	1	cup	*white sugar*
	1	cup	*brown sugar*
	1	cup	*butter,* melted
	2	teaspoons	*cinnamon*

Blend together well. It will be lumpy. Store in refrigerator or freezer for other uses.

*Note from Cat: In selecting which nut (pecan or walnut) to add to a recipe, consider that pecans have a buttery, rich flavor, while walnuts are more bitter.

COCONUT OATMEAL COOKIES

In mixer bowl, combine...	1½	cup	*butter or margarine*
	1½	cup	*brown sugar*
	¾	cup	*white sugar*
Beat until very light and fluffy (it will look like frosting).			

Add...	3	large	*eggs*
	1½	teaspoon	*vanilla extract*
	½	teaspoon	*coconut extract*
Beat well.			

In another bowl, combine...	3	cups	*oats*
	2¼	cups	*flour*
	1	tablespoon	*cinnamon*
	1½	teaspoons	*baking soda*
	½	teaspoon	*salt*
Blend together well.			

Stir in...	1½	cups	*raisins*
	1½	cups	*sweetened coconut*
	1	cup	*walnuts,* chopped

Using a 4 ounce ice cream scoop, portion out cookie dough onto a baking sheet lined with parchment paper. Flatten mounds of dough slightly with palm of your hand. Bake in a **preheated** 325° oven for 14 minutes. **Don't overbake. These will look slightly under-done. They are not!**

Remove from oven. Allow to cool slightly on baking sheet before removing to cooling rack. Let cool completely before wrapping or storing in tight fitting container.

*Walking around an art fair in Jackson one summer day I chanced upon Corey Milligan's **New West Knifeworks*** booth, where he was 'luring' customers into his booth with homemade salsa and chips. Since I was pretty hungry (and I love salsa) I was easy pickins'. Wow! It was the best salsa I'd ever tasted. Really different too. I returned to his booth many times that day....*

Besides purchasing one of his beautiful, inlaid wood knives as a Christmas present for my parents....I also asked for his recipe to put in my book. And here it is!

NEW WEST SALSA

Dice very small... (smaller the better)			
	5	whole	*roma tomatoes*
	1	whole	*cucumber,* peeled
	5	whole	*green onions*
	1	whole	*granny smith apple* peeled & seeded
	1	whole	*red pepper,* seeded
	$1/2$	cup	*red onion*

In mixing bowl, combine above ingredients and add...			
	1	cup	*frozen corn*
	1	cup	*fresh cilantro,* chopped
	$1/4$ +	cup	*canned jalapeno,* diced
	$1/4$ to $1/2$	cup	*fresh lime juice* (to taste)
	2	tablespoons	*balsamic vinegar*
	1	tablespoon	*sugar*
	1	tablespoon	*fresh ground pepper* (to taste)
	1	tablespoon	*salt* (to taste)

You can also use a food processor; however, do each vegetable separately. DON'T over chop!

If you would like to see Corey's beautiful knives, go to his webpage: www.newwestknifeworks.com; or call him toll free 1-877-258-0100.

Dan Hardy is a chef at Signal Mountain Lodge in Grand Teton National Park. After dining at the Lodge this past summer, I invited Dan to share the recipe for the entree I enjoyed so much [you will find that recipe with the Lodge's recipes]. Dan was so enthusiastic about sharing his recipes, that I asked him to share other recipes of his own in this 'Great Cooks' section.

DUCK BREAST with MARIONBERRY
GINGER PORT SAUCE
Serves 6

For this recipe, you will need...	6		**boneless duck breasts,** trimmed, scored
Prepare a marinade of...	1	cup	**red wine**
	$^1/_4$	cup	**fresh orange juice**
	$^1/_4$	cup	**vegetable oil**
	$^1/_2$	tablespoon	**fresh basil,** chopped
	$^1/_2$	tablespoon	**fresh basil,** chopped
Place ducks in marinade for 24 hours.			
In hot skillet, in small amount of oil, pan sear on both sides...			**duck breasts**
Remove from skillet and place in **preheated** 350° oven for about 15 minutes to finish.			
In same skillet, over medium heat, add...	2	teaspoons	**vegetable oil**
	2	tablespoons	**fresh ginger,** minced
	1	teaspoon	**shallots,** minced
Sauté until shallots are translucent.			
Add...	3	cups	**port**
Reduce by a third.			
Add...	1	cup	**marionberries**
	2	cups	**duck or beef stock***
Reduce by half.			

Place sauce in food processor. Puree,
    then strain. Whisk in...   **2**   **tablespoons**   *butter,* broken into
                                                     pieces

To serve, drape duck with sauce. Serve with **Gorgonzola Scallop Potatoes**.

Homemade is always best (see index for recipe); or good quality canned consommé.

GORGONZOLA SCALLOPED POTATOES   Serves 6-8

In large bowl, toss together...	**4** **medium**	*potatoes,* sliced $1/8$" thick
	$^1/_4$ **cup**	*flour*
	1 **tablespoon**	*thyme*
		salt and pepper to taste
Add and toss some more...	**1** **cup**	*heavy cream*

To complete recipe, you will need...	**1** **cup**	*gorgonzola cheese,** crumbled
	$^3/_4$ **cup**	*cornmeal*

Oil small casserole dish. Place single layer of potatoes in bottom; sprinkle with *gorgonzola cheese.* Continue layering potatoes and cheese until all are used, ending with cheese layer. Sprinkle top with *cornmeal.* Cover with foil and bake in **preheated** 350° oven for 1 hour. Remove foil and bake an additional 15 minutes to brown top.

*Blue cheese is an acceptable substitution.

One of my very best friends in the world, Deborah Johnston (also my sister-in-law!) taught me how to make soup. When I started Cafe Christine 16 years ago, soup was not my forte, to put it gently. Deborah was my partner in the Cafe in the very beginning, until career opportunities beckoned my brother to California. Before Deborah left Jackson to join him, she made sure I knew how to make good soup. Now, I can happily say, Deborah and Chuck are back home in Wyoming! Here is the delicious soup I enjoyed in their home most recently.

CRAB CHOWDER

Be sure to buy King Crab Legs (fresh or frozen) and extract the meat from them for this recipe. Whatever you do, don't use canned crab meat for this soup. It will ruin it!

In a large soup pot, add...	3	slices	*bacon,* chopped up
Over medium heat, brown bacon. Add...	1	tablespoon	*butter*
	2	medium	*onions,* chopped
	1	cup	*celery,* chopped
	2	cloves	*garlic,* minced
Sauté until onion is translucent.			

Add...	1	51 oz. can	*clams* (with juice)
	1	51 oz. can	*water*
	2	pounds	*King Crab legs,* meat only
	6	large	*red potatoes,* cubed
	2	tablespoons	*basil*
	1	tablespoon	*celery seeds*
	1	tablespoon	*celery salt*
	1	teaspoon	*black pepper*
Bring to a boil; reduce to simmer for 30 minutes, until potatoes are just tender.			

Add...	2	cups	*half and half*

Simmer another 5 minutes. Serve. If you would like to make the soup thicker, mix equal parts flour and water together; stir in $1/4$ to $1/3$ cup of this mixture to soup. Simmer another 10-12 minutes to the consistency desired.

Variation: Add a cup of fresh corn which has been cooked on the cob and cut off.

JoAnn and I had our daughters 14 days apart and became very good friends over the next couple of years. We found we had lot in common....among other things, our mutual love of good food, and the fact that JoAnn also had her own restaurant in Los Angeles, California. I have enjoyed many wonderful meals in JoAnn's home, including the salmon entree below. It is delicious, and so simple to make.

POACHED SALMON
with STRAWBERRY SAUCE
Serves 4

In covered baking dish with rack, add...	$^1/_2$	cup	*white wine*
	2	cubes	*chicken bouillon*
	2	whole	*bay leaves*
			enough water to barely touch the bottom of rack

On top of rack, place...	4	6 ounce	*fresh salmon filets*
Over salmon, squeeze...	2	wedges	*lemon*

Cover dish and bake in **preheated** 350° oven for 20-30 minutes (depending on thickness of filets), until salmon turns a fleshy pink color and feels firm to the touch.

To serve, remove skin from salmon filets before placing on dinner plates. Spoon Stawberry Sauce over the top of each salmon filet.

Strawberry Sauce

In sauce pan, combine...	2	tablespoons	*soy sauce*
	2	tablespoons	*pure maple syrup*
	$^1/_4$	cup	*strawberry jam*

Heat ingredients, then whisk into a thick glaze.

CHOCOLATE PECAN FLOURLESS TORTE

In double boiler, melt together...	2	ounces	*semi-sweet chocolate*
	2	ounces	*unsweetened chocolate*
	$1/2$	cup	*butter*
Allow to cool slightly.			

In large mixing bowl, whisk together for 1 minute...	3	large	*egg yolks*
	$1/2$	cup	*sugar*
While whisking, slowly add...			*melted chocolate*

In mixing bowl, beat at high speed until soft peaks form...	4	large	*egg whites*
Add...	$1/3$	cup	*sugar*
Beat until stiff.			

Fold half of egg white mixture into chocolate mixture. Then fold in remaining half.

Stir in...	$3/4$	cup	*pecans,* chopped

Pour into greased 8" springform pan. Bake in **preheated** 350° oven for 20 minutes.

Serve with a puree of...	*fresh strawberries*
Garnish with...	*whipped cream*

Always cheerful, with a beautiful smile on her face and a sparkle in her eyes, Karen is a most gracious hostess. Since establishing Incredible Edibles in 1985, she has kept very busy catering dinners and affairs of all sizes. Here are a couple of dishes you might find on her menu at a summer barbeque.

GRILLED SEA BASS with TROPICAL SALSA   Serves 6

"Colorful salsas and relishes made with fresh fruits, vegetables and herbs became popular in this decade of healthful diets. This salsa is light and fresh and packed with flavor that is just right with grilled sea bass." Karen Martin

For this recipe, you will need...	6	6 ounce	*sea bass filets*
			olive oil
			salt and pepper

Brush fillets with oil; sprinkle with salt and pepper. Preheat barbeque to medium-high heat. Grill sea bass until just opaque in center, about 5 minutes per side. Transfer to plates. Top with Tropical Salsa and serve.

Tropical Salsa

Cut into $1/4$" pieces and place in medium bowl...	1	cup	*fresh pineapple,* peeled, cored
	$3/4$	cup	*fresh mango,* peeled, cored
	$2/3$	cup	*red bell pepper,* peeled, cored
	$1/2$	cup	*tomato,* seeded
	$1/3$	cup	*English hothouse cucumber,* seeded
	$1/3$	cup	*red onion*
Add...	3	tablespoons	*fresh cilantro,* minced
	2	tablespoons	*fresh mint,* minced
	2	tablespoons	*fresh jalapeno,* seeded, minced
	2	tablespoons	*fresh lime juice*
			salt to taste

Toss to blend.

Chill to blend flavors, at least 1 hour and up to 4 hours, tossing occasionally.

BEAN-THREAD NOODLE and VEGETABLE SALAD

In large non-stick skillet, over medium high heat, add...	1	tablespoon	*vegetable oil*
When oil is hot, add...	1	pound	*shitake mushrooms,* stems removed, thinly sliced

Sauté mushrooms, stirring frequently, until just tender, about 5 minutes. Place on platter, in one layer, to chill in refrigerator for 15 minutes, or until cool.

In saucepan, bring to a boil...	6	cups	*water*
Remove pan from heat.			
Stir in...	1/2	pound	*bean-thread noodles* (cellophane)

Soak noodles for 15 minutes; drain well in colander. With scissors, cut into 6" lengths.

While noodles are soaking, combine in large bowl...	1¹/2	pounds	*Napa cabbage,* finely shredded (1/2 medium head)
	1/4	pound	*snow peas,* trimmed diagonally, cut into slivers
	1	large	*red bell pepper,* julienned
	3	medium	*carrots,* julienned (2 cups)
	4	whole	*scallions,* sliced thin

Add and toss together with **Dressing**...			*shitake mushrooms cellophane noodles*
Serve salad sprinkled with...	1	teaspoon	*sesame seeds,* toasted*

Toast seeds to golden brown in skillet over medium high heat. Shake, toss or stir sesame seeds continuously until all are golden. Allow to cool before using.

Dressing

In small saucepan, combine...	$1/2$	cup	*soy sauce*
	$1/3$	cup	*water*
	3	tablespoons	*fresh lemon juice*
	2	tablespoons	*sherry*
	1	tablespoon	*distilled vinegar*
	1	tablespoon	*cornstarch*
	1	tablespoon	*sugar*
	1	tablespoon	*fresh ginger,* peeled, grated
	2	cloves	*garlic,* minced

Stirring, bring dressing
to a boil. Reduce to simmer,
stirring constantly 1 minute.

Cool dressing completely, and
stir in... $1^1/2$ teaspoons   *Asian sesame oil*

Dressing may be made two days ahead and chilled, covered.

ASIAN COLESLAW

In large bowl, combine...	5	cups	*green cabbage,* shredded
	2	cups	*red cabbage,* shredded
	2	whole	*red bell peppers,* seeded, thinly sliced
	2	medium	*carrots,* julienned
	6	whole	*green onions,* chopped
	$1/2$	cup	*fresh cilantro,* chopped

Toss with **Dressing** and season with...

*salt and pepper
to taste*
toasted sesame seeds
(optional)

Dressing

In bowl, whisk together...

6	tablespoons	*rice wine vinegar*
6	tablespoons	*vegetable oil*
5	tablespoons	*peanut butter*
		(smooth style)
3	tablespoons	*soy sauce*
3	tablespoons	*brown sugar*
2	tablespoons	*fresh ginger,* minced
1$\frac{1}{2}$	tablespoons	*garlic,* minced

Mary Koontz is the Pastry Chef at The Range. While we were discussing which of her recipes to include as the dessert courses for The Range's two menus in the book, she had so many tempting desserts, it was hard to pick only two. So I asked if she would like to share one more with us.

CHOCOLATE CREME BRULEE
with CHOCOLATE HAZELNUT BISCOTTI

In heavy sauce pan, combine...	$4^1/_2$	cups	*heavy cream*
	$^3/_4$	cup	*sugar*
Bring just to a boil. Remove from heat and add... Let stand 3-5 minutes until melted. Whisk smooth.	15	ounces	*bittersweet chocolate*

In mixing bowl, whisk...	10	large	*egg yolks*

To complete recipe, you will need...	$^3/_4$	cup	*sugar*

Whisk chocolate mixture into egg yolks. Strain into gratin dish. Bake in water bath (with water half way up the gratin dish) in **preheated** 300° oven for about one hour until done (toothpick inserted in center should come out clean). Remove from oven and refrigerate for 4 hours. Just before serving, sprinkle $^3/_4$ cup sugar over the top and brown it with a torch.* Serve with Chocolate Hazelnut Biscotti. Fresh raspberries would be delicious too.

Culinary torches are available in most kitchen/culinary stores or catalogs.

Chocolate Hazelnut Biscotti

In mixing bowl, mix together...	$4^1/_4$	cups	*flour*
	2	cups	*sugar*
	$^1/_2$	cup	*cocoa powder* (unsweetened)
	$^1/_4$	teaspoon	*baking powder*
	$^1/_8$	teaspoon	*ginger*
	$^1/_8$	teaspoon	*salt*

Add...	6	large	*eggs*
	1/4	teaspoon	*vanilla*
Mix until well blended.			

Add and mix well...	1	cup	*chocolate chips*
	2 2/3	cups	*hazelnuts,* roasted* and chopped

Form dough into a flat, log-like loaf onto a cookie sheet. Bake in **preheated** 325° oven for 30 minutes. Remove from oven and allow to cool. Cut into biscotti shapes; place back on cookie sheet and bake again in **preheated** 300° oven for about 5-8 minutes. Remove and allow to cool before serving.

*To roast nuts, place on baking sheet in **preheated** 400° oven for about 8-10 minutes. The nuts are roasted when they start 'popping' and splitting open slightly. Be careful not to burn them!*

As my chef at Cafe Christine during the final three years, Mike Tepe was largely responsible for the success we enjoyed. His knowledge and creativity with food is outstanding. He taught me so much! Mike was always, and is now, a kind and very special friend.

BUTTERNUT and CARROT SOUP   Serves 6

Roast in **preheated** 350° oven for 30 minutes...	2 whole	*butternut squash,* cut in half
Allow to cool; scoop out pulp and coarsely chop.		

In large pot, combine...	1 tablespoon	*butter,* melted
		chopped butternut squash
	1/2 cup	*leek,* chopped
	4 large	*carrots,* chopped
Over medium heat, cook (sweat) the vegetables until leeks are translucent.		

Add...	7 cups	*water*
	7 cups	*chicken broth*
	3/4 teaspoon	*thyme*
	1/4 teaspoon	*nutmeg*
Bring to a boil and let simmer until carrots and squash are soft. Puree in processor or blender.		

Return puree to pot and add...	3 tablespoons	*roasted red pepper,* chopped
	3 tablespoons	*sour cream*
	2 tablespoons	*sherry*
Simmer for 10 minutes.		

Season to taste with...		*salt and pepper*
Garnish with...		*walnuts,* finely chopped

PORK TENDERLOIN
with TOMATO and ANISE   Serves 6

| In a hot skillet, heat... | 1 | tablespoon | *olive oil* |
| Add... | 2 | pounds | *pork tenderloin,* fat and silverskin removed |

Sear on all sides. Set aside.

In same pan, add...	3/4	cup	*red onion,* chopped
	1	teaspoon	*garlic,* minced
	1/2	teaspoon	*anise*

Over medium heat, sauté onion until translucent.

Add...			*port tenderloin*
	1/4	cup	*white wine*
	6	whole	*roma tomatoes,* seeded, diced
	1/2	teaspoon	*fresh rosemary leaves*
	1/2	teaspoon	*fresh thyme leaves*

Simmer for 5 minutes.

| Add... | 2 | tablespoons | *heavy cream* |

Simmer for 1-2 minutes more.

| Season to taste with... | | | *salt and pepper* |
| Garnish with... | | | *black olives,* coarsely chopped |

A very good friend of mine, Moira Cisco, helped me get my restaurant off the gr
Since then I have enjoyed her cooking on many occasions. Here is one of her recipe.
of mine. Great for entertaining or potluck dinners. Be sure to make your own sa.   *Moria's*
recipe...it's great!

CISCO CHICKEN ENCHILADA CASSEROLE
with FRESH SALSA
Serves 8

For this recipe, you will need...	3	**pounds**	*chicken meat,* poached, shredded
	18		*corn tortillas*
In large sauce pan, combine...	2	**tablespoons**	*vegetable oil*
	1	**large**	*onion,* chopped
Sauté until onion is soft.			
Add...	1	**cup**	*half and half*
	1	**cup**	*chicken broth* (canned)
	2	**12 oz. cans**	*green enchilada sauce*
	2	**cups**	*monterey jack cheese,* shredded
Stir until melted.			
Add and mix well...			*shredded chicken*
	1/4	**cup** (packed)	*fresh cilantro,* chopped
To complete recipe, you will need...	1	**cup**	*sharp cheddar cheese,* grated

In bottom of greased 3 quart casserole dish, spread one layer of *corn tortillas*. Spoon about one third of chicken mixture evenly over the top. Continue alternating layers of tortillas and chicken mixture, ending with the chicken. Top with shredded *sharp cheddar cheese*. Bake in **preheated** 300° oven until heated through, approximately 40 minutes. Serve with sour cream and fresh Salsa.

Salsa

In a bowl, combine...			
	1	can (drained)	*Rotele Original* Tomatoes & Green Chilis*
	1	can (drained)	*Rotele Milder* Tomatoes & Green Chilis*
	4	ripe	*roma tomatoes,* diced small
	1	large	*white onion,* chopped
	¹/₂	cup (packed)	*fresh cilantro,* chopped
	¹/₂ to 1	whole	*lime,* juice of
	1	teaspoon	*garlic salt*
	1	cup	*cucumber,* diced (optional)
	1	8 oz can	*white corn,* drained (optional)

*You'll find these in every large grocery store.

Over the years, Neal Starrett has been pastry chef for both the Blue Lion and Off Broadway restaurants in Jackson. Though he is now following other business pursuits, he still loves to bake! Here is just a sampling.

BUTTERMILK PIE with RHUBARB COMPOTE

| For this recipe, you will need... | 1 | unbaked | *pie crust* |
| | | | (in shallow 9" pan) |

| In mixing bowl, combine... | 1¼ | cups | *sugar* |
| | 3 | tablespoons | *flour* |

| Add and mix thoroughly... | 4 | large | *eggs* |

Stir in...	4	ounces	*butter,* melted
	1	cup	*buttermilk*
	1		*fresh lemon,* zest of
	1	tablespoon	*fresh lemon juice*
	1	teaspoon	*vanilla extract*
	1	pinch	*nutmeg*

Mix thoroughly.

Pour into unbaked pie crust. Bake in **preheated** 350° oven for 45-55 minutes, until browned and firm in center. Remove from oven and cool to room temperature. Serve with **Rhubarb Compote.**

Rhubarb Compote

In sauce pan, combine...	12-15	ribs	*rhubarb,* washed, trimmed and cut into 1" sections
	1½	cups	*sugar*
	⅛	cup	*water*

Simmer until thickened. Cool and serve with room temperature Buttermilk Pie.

TIRAMISU

Serves 8-10

This melt-in-your-mouth dessert requires five steps....a four-part preparation and final assemply....but well worth the effort. What a way to wow friends and influence enemies! Neal's interpretation of this yummy dessert is one of the best!

Step 1 — Genoise

In large bowl, whisk together...	1/3	cup	*unsweetened cocoa*
	1/4	cup	*boiling water*
Set aside.			

In another bowl, place...	5	large	*eggs*
Place this bowl over simmering water to warm eggs until just warm to the touch.			

In mixer bowl, combine...			*warmed eggs*
	1/4	cup	*sugar*
Whip on high speed until eggs have reached full volume. Remove 1 cup and fold it into *cocoa mixture* with...	1	teaspoon	*vanilla extract*

To remainder of egg in bowl, carefully fold in...	3/4	cup	*cake flour,* sifted before measuring

Add cocoa/egg mixture to flour/egg mixture. Fold in...	1 1/2	ounces	*clarified butter,* kept warm

Pour into 10" cake pan which has been greased and floured. Bake in **preheated** 350° oven for 22-25 minutes until done (toothpick inserted will come out clean). Cool.

Step 2 — Mascarpone Filling

In mixer bowl, place...	1	pound	*cream cheese*

Beat cream cheese until smooth, scraping down sides often to get rid of any lumps.

When smooth, add...	5	tablespoons	*sour cream*

Mix thoroughly, scraping sides down often.

Slowly, add...	1	cup	*heavy cream*
Add...	2	tablespoons	*sugar*

Set aside.

Step 3 — Espresso Mixture

In small bowl, mix together...	1	cup	*freshly brewed espresso*
	1/2	cup	*rum* (dark or light)
	6	tablespoons	*sugar*
	2	teaspoons	*vanilla extract*

Set aside.

Step 4 — Zabaglione

In stainless mixing bowl, combine...	6	large	*egg yolks*
	6	tablespoons	*sugar*
	6	tablespoons	*marsala*

Set bowl over pan of simmering water. Whisk constantly until thick and smooth. Set aside.

Step 5 — ASSEMBLY

• After genoise has cooled, with a cake cutter or sharp serrated bread knife, carefully cut the cake in three even layers. A round stiff piece of cardboard will help to transfer the slices.

• Place one slice of *Genoise* into bottom of 10" springform pan. Brush top with *Espresso Mixture* until a third of it is used up. Next, spread half the *Mascarpone Filling* over top, followed by a third of the *Zabaglione.*

• Repeat the layers, beginning with another slice of the Genoise, brush it with a third of *Espresso*, followed by the other half of *Mascarpone* and a third of *Zabaglione.*

• Place the final layer of *Genoise* on top, soak it with the remaining *Espresso* and then the last of the *Zabaglione.* Cover with plastic and refrigerate.

Before serving, dust with...

unsweetened cocoa
chopped almonds

Remove sides of springform pan. Slice!

When the lower level of the Mangy Moose was first developed years ago, there was a tiny dessert shop called Just Desserts in the Rocky Mountain Oyster. Sue Euler was the baker for six years. Her desserts were a big hit. They sold literally thousands of her Fudge Bars. So, for those of you who have always wanted to know how to make them, here's the recipe!

FUDGE BARS   Makes about 12 Bars

In large mixing bowl, combine...	3	cups	*flour*
	1³/₄	cups	*brown sugar*
	1	cup	*margarine or butter*
	3	large	*eggs*
	1¹/₂	teaspoons	*baking soda*
	1	tablespoon	*vanilla*

Beat at low speed until well mixed, occasionally scraping the bowl. Increase to medium speed and beat 3 minutes, occasionally scraping bowl.

Gently add...	2	cups	*oatmeal*
	1¹/₂	cups	*pecans,* chopped
Set aside.			

In heavy saucepan, over low heat, combine...	12	ounces	*semi-sweet chocolate chips*
	14	ounces	*sweetened condensed milk*
	3	tablespoons	*butter*
Stir occasionally, until melted and mixture is smooth.			

| Remove from heat. Stir in... | ³/₄ | cup | *pecans,* chopped |
| | 1 | tablespoon | *vanilla* |

Press half of oatmeal dough into 9" x 13" greased and floured pan. Spread chocolate mixture over dough. Drop remaining oatmeal dough by spoonfuls to cover chocolate mixture (some chocolate should show through). Bake in **preheated** 350° oven for 45 minutes. Top should be lightly golden. Cool completely in pan on wire rack. Cut into bars.

COCONUT GOO-GOO BARS

Makes about 12 Bars

In mixer bowl, combine...	1	cup	*butter,* softened
	$^2/_3$	cup	*white sugar*
	$^2/_3$	cup	*brown sugar*

Cream together until fluffy
and light, about 2-3 minutes.

| Add and beat well... | 2 | large | *eggs* |
| | 2 | teaspoons | *vanilla extract* |

| In small bowl, combine... | $2^1/_4$ | cups | *flour* |
| | 1 | teaspoon | *baking soda* |

On low speed, add this to
the sugar-egg mixture. Beat
until just combined.

Stir into batter...	$2^1/_2$	cups	*sweetened coconut flakes*
	$1^1/_2$	cups	*semi-sweet chocolate chips*
	1	cup	*pecans,* chopped

Spread finished batter into greased and floured 9" x 9" baking pan. Bake in **preheated** 350° oven for 20-25 minutes, or until golden (toothpick in center should come out slightly moist). DO NOT overbake. Cool completely in pan on wire rack. Cut into bars.

*Tim Labassi, chef for the Blue Lion in Jackson, is also the creator of **Fish Creek Foods**, a line of spicy sauces, salsas, chutneys and pestos. His spicy concoctions range from mild to hot, and they are scrumptious! Here is a spicy pineapple relish created with his Pineapple Habanero Hot Sauce.**

JAMAICAN SHRIMP   Serves 8

Peel and devein...	2-3	pounds	*large shrimp*
In bowl, combine shrimp with... Let stand for 30 minutes.			**Red Pepper Habanero Sauce**
In large sauté pan, combine...	$^1/_2$	whole	*pineapple,* diced
	$^3/_4$	cup	*red pepper,* diced
	$^1/_2$	cup	*red onion,* diced
	2	teaspoons	*garlic,* minced
Sauté 2 minutes.			
Add and simmer over low heat, covered, for about 15 minutes...	5	ounces	*Pineapple Habanero Hot Sauce*
Allow to cool and add...	3	tablespoons	*fresh cilantro,* chopped
	3	ounces	*pineapple juice*

Grill shrimp until done (when the seam along the back has just turned white, they are perfect). Remove from heat immediately. Serve with pineapple relish.

*If you don't live in Jackson and you would like to have some of his wonderful sauces, visit his website: www.fishcreekfoods.com; or call toll free 1-888-799-7782.

Todd Baron is a chef at Signal Mountain Lodge in Grand Teton National Park. He created the terrific entree, Trout with Sundried Tomato-Raspberry Vinaigrette, which my friend enjoyed when we dined at the Lodge this past summer. You will find that recipe with the Lodge's recipes in this book. Todd was very happy to share another with us!

GRILLED HALIBUT on GOLDEN MOLE SAUCE with SALSA FRESCA and BLACK BEANS
Serves 6

For this recipe, you will need...	6	6-8 ounce	*halibut filets*
			olive oil
			salt and pepper

Brush *halibut filets* with *olive oil* and season with *salt and pepper*. Grill over medium high heat until just done, about 4-5 minutes on each side.

Serve halibut on top of Golden Mole Sauce. Drape with Salsa Fresca and serve with black beans.

Golden Mole Sauce

In large sauté pan, combine...	4	tablespoons	*corn oil*
	¹/₂	cup	*sunflower seeds* (unsalted)
	4	cloves	*garlic,* minced
	4	large	*yellow bell peppers* seeded, chopped
	1	large	*white onion,* chopped
	1	tablespoon	*cumin*
	1	teaspoon	*cinnamon*
	1	teaspoon	*salt*

Sauté all ingredients together until onions are translucent.

| Add... | 3 | cups | *chicken broth* (canned) |

Simmer for 20 minutes on lowest heat. Puree smooth and hold warm.

Salsa Fresca

In bowl, combine and mix well...

1	whole	*lime,* juice of
6	large	*roma tomatoes,* diced
1/4	cup	*red onion,* diced small
1/4	cup	*fresh cilantro,* chopped
3	tablespoons	*olive oil*
1	teaspoon	*salt*
1	pinch	*black pepper*

Can be made one day ahead. Store, covered, in refrigerator. Serve at room temperature.

CHICKEN STOCK
Makes 2 Quarts

Canned chicken stock tends to be too salty. It doesn't really take much effort to produce your own rich chicken stock for flavoring sauces and soups.

In stock pot, combine...

4	pounds	*chicken parts* (backs, wings, necks)
6	quarts	*water*
2	medium	*carrots,* chopped
1	large	*onion,* chopped
1	rub	*celery,* chopped
1	whole	*bay leaf*
2	teaspoons	*thyme*
1	teaspoon	*black peppercorns*
3	whole	*cloves*
3	sprigs	*parsley*

Over medium high heat, bring to a boil. As the stock comes to a boil, foam will appear on top. Skim off the foam. Reduce heat to lowest temperature. Simmer for 3 to 4 hours, until liquid is reduced by half. Strain stock through a fine sieve (lined with cheesecloth, if you have it; this will produce a clearer stock). Allow stock to cool to room temperature uncovered. Then cover and refrigerate until ready to use. If you don't plan to use the stock within 2 to 3 days, freeze it.

BEEF/VEAL STOCK
Makes 2 Quarts

Get beef or veal bones from your butcher. Leg bones with the joints are best so there will be plenty of marrow to flavor the stock. Make sure he cuts them up into manageable size pieces for your stock pot.

On baking sheet, place...

4	pounds	*beef or veal bones*
2	medium	*onions,* halved

Bake in a **preheated** 375° oven for 45 minutes, until well browned.

In stock pot, combine...

		browned bones
		roasted onions
6	quarts	*water*
2	medium	*tomatoes,* chopped
1	large	*carrot,* chopped
1	rib	*celery,* chopped
1	whole	*bay leaf*
1	teaspoon	*thyme*
1	teaspoon	*black peppercorns*
6	whole	*cloves*
3	sprigs	*parsley*
3	cups	*red wine* (optional)

Over medium high heat, bring to a boil. As the stock comes to a boil, foam will appear on top. Skim off the foam. Reduce heat to lowest temperature. Simmer for at least 8 hours. The longer you simmer it, the better it will be. Simmering for 12 hours or overnight is ideal. Strain stock through a fine sieve (lined with cheesecloth, if you have it; this will produce a clearer stock). Allow stock to cool to room temperature uncovered. Then cover and refrigerate until ready to use. If you don't plan to use the stock within 2 to 3 days, freeze it.

DEMI-GLACE

In large saucepan, bring to a boil...	2 quarts	*homemade beef stock*

Turn heat to lowest temperature and reduce stock to about 1 to 2 cups demi-glace. It has reduced to a demi-glace if it thoroughly coats the back of a spoon. Be sure to remove any scum which accumulates on the surface as it is simmering. The reduction will take several hours to complete.

Short-Cut Substitutions

Not nearly as good as the real thing, but helpful in a pinch.

- In saucepan, over lowest heat, reduce by half a good quality, canned beef consommé.

- Dissolve 2 teaspoons beef base in 2 tablespoons red wine.

INDEX

See also RECIPE BY MENU CATEGORY,

creme brulee, 159, 239
crepe, 147
CUSTARD
  caramel, huckleberry, 64
  chocolate creme brulee, 239
  creme brulee, 159
  russian cream, 24
  tiramisu, 246
  zabaglione, 40

D
demi-glace, 255
DESSERTS
  See *Recipe by Menu Category*
DRESSING
  Asian, 237
  balsamic, 21, 37, 132
  caesar, 66, 205
  champagne, 156
  chardonnay, 119
  citrus-chive, 137
  Italian, 14
  lemon tarragon, 92
  maple raspberry, 164
  orange ginger, 86
  oriental, 203
  poppy seed, 204
  portabello, 58
  sesame Orange, 151
  Sundried Tomato, 107, 193
  wasabi, 106
duck, 29, 171, 230

E
eggplant, 137
elk, 108, 120
ENTREES
  See *Recipe by Menu Category*

F
FISH
  See *Seafood*
flan, corn, 157
fruit salad, 20
fudge bars, 249

G
gazpacho, 163
goat cheese, 43, 121, 137, 221
gorgonzola, 113, 132, 144

H
halibut, 157, 252
HUCKLEBERRY
  chocolate paté, 81
  cobbler, 24
  creme caramel, 64
  stuffing, 56
  zabaglione, 40

I
ice cream, 8, 122
Italian dressing, 14

J
jalapeno, 189, 226

K
Kahlua, bread pudding, 217

L
lamb, 44, 94
limoncello, 101
linguini, 15

M
marinara sauce, 12
mayonnaise, 197
minestrone, 13
mint sauce, 94
miso soup, 5, 184
muffins, 181, 227
MUSHROOM
  polenta, 171
  portabello, 58
  shitake, 5, 23, 125
  strudel, 93
  wild, 38, 113, 171
mussels, 43, 74

N
nage, corn, 138

O
onion, 36
oysters. 19

P
PANCAKES
  sweet potato, 56
  white corn, 162
  roesti, 146

Please send me copies of *A Taste of Jackson Hole II* at $19.50 per copy. For shipping and handling, I am enclosing $2.75 for the first book, and $1.50 for each additional book.

Cost for Cookbook(s) $_____

Shipping/Handling $_____

Total Amont Enclosed $_____

Make check or money order payable **Christine Goodman.** Send order to:

**Christine Goodman
P.O. Box 3308
Jackson, Wyoming 83001**

Ship to _____

Address _____

City _____ State _____ Zip _____

Please send me copies of *A Taste of Jackson Hole II* at $19.50 per copy. For shipping and handling, I am enclosing $2.75 for the first book, and $1.50 for each additional book.

Cost for Cookbook(s) $_____

Shipping/Handling $_____

Total Amont Enclosed $_____

Make check or money order payable **Christine Goodman.** Send order to:

**Christine Goodman
P.O. Box 3308
Jackson, Wyoming 83001**

Ship to _____

Address _____

City _____ State _____ Zip _____

Please send me copies of *A Taste of Jackson Hole II* at $19.50 per copy. For shipping and handling, I am enclosing $2.75 for the first book, and $1.50 for each additional book.

Cost for Cookbook(s) $_____

Shipping/Handling $_____

Total Amont Enclosed $_____

Make check or money order payable **Christine Goodman.** Send order to:

**Christine Goodman
P.O. Box 3308
Jackson, Wyoming 83001**

Ship to _____

Address _____

City _____ State _____ Zip _____